REGENTS CRITICS SERIES

General Editor: Paul A. Olson

# LITERARY CRITICISM OF
# JOHN DRYDEN

Other volumes of the Regents Critics Series are:

# Literary Criticism of John Dryden

*Edited by*

ARTHUR C. KIRSCH

UNIVERSITY OF NEBRASKA PRESS · LINCOLN

MANUFACTURED IN THE UNITED STATES OF AMERICA

# Regents Critics Series

The Regents Critics Series provides reading texts of significant literary critics in the Western tradition. The series treats criticism as a useful tool: an introduction to the critic's own poetry and prose if he is a poet or novelist, an introduction to other work in his day if he is more judge than creator. Nowhere is criticism regarded as an end in itself but as what it is—a means to the understanding of the language of art as it has existed and been understood in various periods and societies.

Each volume includes a scholarly introduction which describes how the work collected came to be written, and suggests its uses. All texts are edited in the most conservative fashion consonant with the production of a good reading text; and all translated texts observe the dictum that the letter gives life and the spirit kills when a technical or rigorous passage is being put into English. Other types of passages may be more freely treated. Footnoting and other scholarly paraphernalia are restricted to the essential minimum. Such features as a bibliographical checklist are carried where they are appropriate to the work in hand. If a volume is the first collection of the author's critical writing, this is noted in the bibliographical data.

PAUL A. OLSON

University of Nebraska

# Contents

# Introduction

Dryden's criticism is easy to undervalue or to value for the wrong reasons. To be truly understood it must be accepted on its own terms, and at a distance of two centuries those terms are neither easy to perceive nor appreciate. All critics suffer from such historical accidents, but Dryden does especially, for he is very unlike what we currently expect a critic to be. He neither analyzes a text intensively nor speaks portentously about literary form or theory. His criticism is almost entirely occasional: prefaces, dedications, prologues, epilogues, written to explain or justify his own works. He changes his mind, often, and has little patience with theoretical positions for their own sake. His interests are practical to the point of being technical. In the modern critical pantheon these are not virtues, and we are tempted to explain them away either by reducing Dryden to an amateur who wrote graceful prose and entertaining shoptalk or by magnifying him into a skeptic who contradicted himself on the basis of consistent philosophical premises. But Dryden was not a philosophical skeptic, and he certainly was no amateur. He was a great literary critic, and it is worth the effort to discover this greatness in qualities which are really his.

To begin with, we must fully appreciate the pragmatic character of his criticism. From 1664, when he published his first critical essay, to 1700, when he published his last, Dryden wrote for a living. For the first fifteen years of his career he was a dramatist (for most of that time under contract to write three plays a year for one of the two theatrical companies in London); and *Of Dramatic Poesy*, "A Defence of *An Essay of Dramatic Poesy*," the "Preface to *An Evening's Love*," the "Heads of an Answer to Rymer," and the "Preface to *Troilus and Cressida* Containing the Grounds of Criticism in Tragedy" all reflect his professional commitment and interest in the contemporary English theater. "An Apology for Heroic Poetry and Heroic Licence" and the "Preface to *Fables*" similarly are the product of

Dryden's later professional interests, in the one case, his experimentation with epic or heroic verse, in the other, his work as a translator. All of the critical essays, with the exception of *Of Dramatic Poesy* and the "Heads of an Answer to Rymer," were published with the works Dryden was attempting to justify or explore; and the exceptions, as we shall see, only prove the rule.

*Of Dramatic Poesy* purports to deal with large and theoretical issues: the Ancients versus the Moderns, the French versus the English, blank verse versus heroic verse; and its dialogue form contributes to a sense of disinterested speculation. But the dice are loaded not merely in the obvious partiality toward Neander, Dryden's spokesman in the discussion, but in the most basic purposes of the essay. For, appearances to the contrary, Dryden does have a stake in the argument: he is concerned with justifying his profession as a dramatist, and this commits him to a general defense of English theatrical conventions against critics who advocated the very different practices of the Greek and Roman or of the French neoclassical theater, and to a specific defense of his own innovation within the English tradition, the use of rhymed rather than blank verse in tragedy. He himself says clearly enough in the brief note to the reader that the purpose of the essay was "to vindicate the honor of our English writers from the censure of those who unjustly prefer the French before them," and his plea for the English dramatic tradition, together with his defense of his own use of rhyme in tragedy, which occupies the final third of the essay, are obvious enough.

Less obvious and equally important are the ways in which various parts of the argument are manipulated to support his practical commitments. The controversy of Ancient versus Modern, for example, which looks like a set piece on the subject and seems irrelevant, is actually designed to qualify the authority of classical drama and hence of its modern derivative, French neoclassical drama. The very definition of a play which the company agrees upon is calculated to serve the English side. But even within the English tradition, Dryden's judgments and argument are affected by his profession. Jonson, who had an exceptionally high reputation in cultivated circles at the time but little popularity and practical effect on the Restoration stage, Dryden treats with reserve. He analyzes Jonson's *Silent Woman* at length, but his purpose is not to do homage to Jonson—still less to analyze the play for its own sake— so much as to use Jonson's classical reputation and practice as a means of making the case for the traditions of English drama even more unassailable. His actual regard for Jonson, here as in all his other essays, is qualified. Fletcher, on the other hand, had the greatest possible effect upon early Restoration drama—as Dryden points out, his and Beaumont's plays being "the most pleasant and frequent entertainments of the stage; two of theirs being acted through the year for every one of Shakespeare's or Jonson's"—and Dryden's treatment of Fletcher is correspondingly appreciative. When Fletcher's popularity on the stage began to decline in the late 1670's, Dryden's estimation of him became somewhat more moderate (compare the discussions of Fletcher in *Of Dramatic Poesy* and in the "Preface to *Troilus and Cressida*"). To Shakespeare Dryden gives his highest praise, at a time when such praise was not yet fashionable, partly because he simply had the taste to recognize Shakespeare's genius, but partly also because that very taste had been formed by his experience with a living English theater in which Shakespeare's influence was powerful, if not always direct or apparent.

Dryden's other essays on the drama are similarly affected by his practice and its circumstances. "A Defence of *An Essay of Dramatic Poesy*" continues his justification of rhyme and contains the kind and detail of argument possible only for a man actively engaged in writing rhymed dramatic verse as well as talking about it. The "Preface to *An Evening's Love*" consists of a defense of repartee in comedy, which Dryden loved and could do well, against Jonsonian humour, which he found uncongenial, and questions Jonson's authority because that authority was being invoked in critical attacks upon his comedies by the contemporary dramatist Thomas Shadwell. The "Heads of an Answer to Rymer" and the "Preface to *Troilus and Cressida*" are both directed against *The Tragedies of the Last Age* (1677), a work by Thomas Rymer which rigorously and destructively applied classical standards of dramatic decorum to early English plays, including those of Shakespeare and Fletcher.

In light of this attack Dryden's immediate and characteristically practical concern was, as he remarked in the "Preface," "to inquire how far we ought to imitate our own poets, Shakespeare and Fletcher, in their tragedies." The inquiry in the "Heads of an Answer to Rymer," which consists of notes Dryden made in his copy of Rymer's book and which was not published until after Dryden's death, is a direct and unequivocal attack upon Rymer's premises and conclusions; the "Preface to *Troilus and Cressida*," which Dryden did publish, is a more circumspect and indirect defense of the English dramatic tradition. But in both cases, whether through attack or insinuation, Dryden's essential argument is that Rymer's strictures, however theoretically consistent or logical, are simply contradicted by the experience of contemporary audiences. In "Heads of an Answer" he goes so far as to suggest that " 'tis not enough that Aristotle has said so, for Aristotle drew his models of tragedy from Sophocles and Euripides; and if he had seen ours, might have changed his mind." This is a revolutionary statement (and one which Dryden never had the courage to pursue in print) but it follows naturally from the consistent priority which he gave to practice over theory.

The same priority is evident in his criticism of poetry. "An Apology for Heroic Poetry and Heroic Licence," though freighted with classical precedents and a more than usual amount of theoretical argument about the nature of decorum, is finally designed to justify his own love and practice of figurative writing and "imaging," which he believed to be "in itself, the very height and life of poetry." The "Preface to *Fables*," his last critical work, is even more obviously the product of his dispositions as a writer. He compares Homer with Virgil, and Chaucer with Ovid and Boccaccio, and he discriminates among them with great judiciousness; but in each case the author whom he admires most, and about whom he has the freshest and most penetrating insights, is the author with whom he himself feels most compatible as a writer: Homer, whose "vehemence" he finds "more suitable" to his "temper," and Chaucer, whose "soul" he finds "congenial" to his own.

So thorough an orientation toward practice, of course, has its drawbacks. Much of Dryden's criticism is occupied with self-justification and even self-advertisement, and many of his more controversial arguments are marked by petty squabbling. Parts of his attack upon Sir Robert Howard are especially unenlightening. Less venial and more complicated are some of the consequences of his practical prejudice against any systematic theory. He seems, for example, to have been unable to cope with Rymer's assault upon the foundations of English drama. That he disagreed with Rymer's myopic criticism is obvious from his comments in "Heads of an Answer"; but it is equally clear that he could not translate that disagreement into any systematic public criticism of Rymer's position. The "Preface to *Troilus and Cressida*" is hesitant, evasive, and finally rather unsatisfying; and significantly it is his most theoretical essay.

Dryden's practical temperament is at least partially responsible for this kind of critical failure. He did not have any considerable ability to formulate theory; he constantly deferred to other critics, especially the French, for analytical discriminations. But the analytical limitations of Dryden's criticism are also partially the inevitable consequence of the state of English criticism at that time. Toward the end of his life Dryden remarked that in his earlier criticism he had had to navigate in an uncharted sea without instruments: "As I may say, before the use of the loadstone, or knowledge of the compass, I was sailing in a vast ocean, without other help, than the polestar of the Ancients, and the rules of the French stage amongst the Moderns, which are extremely different from ours, by reason of their opposite taste . . . ." Dryden exaggerated: Ben Jonson, at least, left a significant legacy of analytical tools, and Dryden himself, as we shall see in a moment, was not without some coherent critical premises to work from. Nevertheless, his complaints about the primitive state of dramatic criticism in England were justified and should be appreciated. Jonson was the only English critic before Dryden ever to have attempted concerted dramatic criticism, and his criticism was disconnected and a half-century old. Dryden therefore often had to create the critical tools, especially a new vocabulary, capable of justifying the nature and aims of contemporary plays; and in so doing he could not always anticipate the implications of the terms and premises he employed. This was probably the reason that Rymer intimidated him, for Rymer used a similar critical language to reach conclusions with which Dryden could not possibly agree. In "Heads of an Answer" Dryden saw what the trouble was—that Rymer was applying to English plays and the English theatrical tradition a terminology which Aristotle had developed inductively through his observation of Greek plays and the Greek theatrical tradition. But Dryden apparently did not feel willing or able to follow that insight to its conclusion and to develop a different and more appropriate critical language. And this is a loss.

On the other hand, it is hardly fatal. Rymer's criticism, for all its analytical stringency, is now only of pedantic interest, whereas Dryden's is alive. And one reason, at least, is that the practical bias which appears to limit Dryden's criticism also gives it a fundamental analytical ballast, namely, the understanding that poetry can be neither created nor criticized without taking account of the responses of its audience. "Delight is the chief, if not the only end of poesy," Dryden remarks in "A Defence of *An Essay*," and his adherence to this principle, born of his practice, produces all that is most original, penetrating, and humane in his criticism. It accounts, for example, for the particularly rich and spacious way in which he followed the polestar of the Ancients, both in his practice and criticism. He writes in "An Apology for Heroic Poetry" that, following Horace and Virgil, he has "made use of the hardest metaphors, and of the strongest hyperboles," because

> in this case the best authority is the best argument. For generally to have pleased, and through all ages, must bear the force of universal tradition. And if you would appeal from thence to right reason, you will gain no more by it in effect than, first, to set up your reason against those authors; and, secondly, against all those who have admired them. You must prove why that ought not to have pleased, which has pleased the most learned and the most judicious; and to be thought knowing, you must first put the fool upon all mankind.

The notion that classical rules and precedents ultimately derive their authority from their ability to please centuries of readers is the root assumption of all neoclassical criticism, from Sir Philip Sidney to Samuel Johnson. But with the exception of Johnson, only in Dryden does that assumption really operate; in the others it is often solely an uncompromising appeal to authority. Dryden loved the classics, deeply and abidingly, and he did not have to be told to emulate them; but he also wrote for a contemporary audience with contemporary tastes. The glory of his criticism, as it is of his poetry, is that he is usually able to do both. On the one hand, he does his best not to pander to popular fashion and is always aware that criticism must be informed by inherited values and standards. This is the deeper burden of his argument with Sir Robert Howard, whose attitude was that criticism was basically a matter of the cultivated taste of gentlemen, anything else being a form of social as well as literary pretense. (The obvious snobbery of this position may account for Dryden's acrimonious tone in "A Defence.") Dryden's answer is that

> The liking or disliking of the people gives the play the denomination of good or bad, but does not really make or constitute it such. To please the people ought to be the poet's aim, because plays are made for their delight; but it does not follow that they are always pleased with good plays, or that plays which please them are always good. The humour of the people is now for comedy, therefore in hope to please them, I write comedies rather than serious plays: and so far their taste prescribes to me: but it does not follow from that reason that comedy is to be preferred before tragedy in its own nature, for that which is so in its own nature cannot be otherwise, as a man cannot but be a rational creature. . . .

Dryden never altered this basic belief in the intrinsic nature of literary genres and standards of decorum inherited from the experience of classical literature, and it gives the stability and coherence of a felt tradition to his criticism and practice.

But on the other hand, his profoundest commitment is always and finally to a living literature and its relation to a living audience, and it is this commitment which most enriches his criticism of both the past and the present. For, given the assumption that a writer must please his audience, it followed, for Dryden, that writers would have to please different audiences in different ways. He saw clearly—and was the first in England to do so—that audiences and the demands they made changed over periods of time and varied in different nations, a perception which, in his practice, balanced his use of tradition, and which, in his criticism, enabled him to have the widest possible imaginative sympathy with the literature of different ages and cultures. *Of Dramatic Poesy*, for example, despite its tendentious argument for the English dramatic tradition, shows an understanding of the peculiar virtues of the French neoclassical theater which was without precedent in English criticism and which has hardly been surpassed since; and there is surely no essay on comparative literature in the English language which can rival the simultaneous partisanship and tolerance of the "Preface to *Fables*."

No English critic can match Dryden in this respect. Many of the greatest are, like him, writers, whose practice enables them to explore literary traditions meaningfully, and whose own creative power endows their criticism with imaginative life (T. S. Eliot is perhaps the closest analogue, both in critical methods and views). But none of them have Dryden's breadth, his extraordinary ability to be nourished by tradition without being inhibited by it, his capacity—amounting to genius—to see for himself and for us at the same time.

## A Note on the Texts

Spelling and punctuation have been modernized for all the selections, and translations are given in the text for all quotations in a foreign language, except when the original is necessary for the point Dryden is making. Unless otherwise indicated, the translations are the editor's. The original quotations are given in the footnotes. Otherwise the texts are faithful transcriptions of the first editions.

There are two authoritative editions of *An Essay of Dramatic Poesy*, the first in 1668, and the second in 1684. Dryden made a number of syntactical changes in the second edition to conform to late Restoration usage, especially in the placement of prepositions. I have used the first edition because on the few occasions where there is a possible modulation of meaning the first edition gives a more accurate picture of the place of the *Essay* in Dryden's critical development. Also, the style of the first edition is frequently more energetic. A modern reprint of the *Essay* based upon the 1684 text has been edited by James T. Bolton (Oxford, 1964).

The "Heads of an Answer to Rymer" also exists in two authoritative texts: in Tonson's edition of the works of Beaumont and Fletcher (1711), and in Johnson's "Life of Dryden" (1779). Both texts were evidently printed from Dryden's manuscript notes in his copy, now lost, of Rymer's *Tragedies of the Last Age*, but the order of the notes is quite different and there are also some verbal variants. I have followed Tonson's text because his order seems more coherent than Johnson's, but in a number of instances I have adopted a verbal variant from Johnson. Johnson's text may be found at the end of his "Life of Dryden," *Lives of the English Poets*, ed. G. B. Hill (Oxford, 1905). For a discussion of the comparative merits of Tonson's and Johnson's texts, see James M. Osborn, *John Dryden: Facts and Problems* (New York, 1940), pp. 267–269.

ARTHUR C. KIRSCH

University of Virginia

# LITERARY CRITICISM OF
# JOHN DRYDEN

# *Of Dramatic Poesy: An Essay*
# (1668)

*Dryden has two basic purposes in this essay: to defend the conventions and traditions of the English stage, and to justify his own use of rhymed heroic verse in tragedy.*

*English drama had come under attack a few years earlier from a Frenchman, Samuel Sorbière, who charged in his* Relation d'un voyage en Angleterre *(1664) that English dramatists failed to observe any of the three classical unities and violated credibility by their disposition to represent violence and improbable actions on stage. His charges were answered by Thomas Sprat in* Observations on Monsieur de Sorbier's Voyage into England *(1665). Dryden makes use of the arguments of both writers in the essay, but his own defense of English drama extends beyond the terms of this specific controversy. Many English critics, including Sidney and Jonson, had been as critical of English stage conventions as Sorbière and, like him, had argued for the kind of focused dramatic illusion which was represented in classical drama. Dryden occasionally accedes to this premise—he tries hard, for example, to prove that English plays can be as classical as the classics—but essentially his argument is designed to support the panoramic illusion of the English stage. In fact, the real force of the* Essay, *and its distinctive contribution to English dramatic criticism, rests precisely in its simple recognition that English drama is different from classical drama, written for a different audience and based upon a different idea of theater, and thus impossible to judge on the basis of standards derived from either classical or French neoclassical practice.*

*The* Essay *also forms a part of another controversy—an extended quarrel with Sir Robert Howard over rhymed dramatic verse. Dryden first defended the use of heroic couplets in serious drama in the preface to* The Rival Ladies *(1664). Howard replied, criticizing the use of rhyme, in the preface to* Four New Plays *(1665). Dryden in turn answered him in the final dialogue of the* Essay *between Crites, who takes Howard's position, and Neander, who takes Dryden's. Howard angrily answered back in the preface*

3

*to* The Great Favorite, or The Duke of Lerma (*1668*), *and Dryden closed the exchange with* "*A Defence of* An Essay of Dramatic Poesy," *which he prefixed to the second edition of his play* The Indian Emperor (*1668*). *The whole quarrel is integrally connected with Dryden's practice and theory of the heroic play and cannot be adequately summarized outside of that context. There is, however, one premise in Dryden's defense of rhyme which can be extrapolated and which is important to notice, and that is his stress upon decorum and the artifice of the imitation itself, rather than upon the illusion of the thing imitated. This emphasis subsumes all of his criticism, and indeed, all of his work.*

## TO THE READER

The drift of the ensuing discourse was chiefly to vindicate the honor of our English writers from the censure of those who unjustly prefer the French before them.[1] This I intimate, lest any should think me so exceeding vain as to teach others an art which they understand much better than myself. But if this incorrect Essay, written in the country without the help of books, or advice of friends, shall find any acceptance in the world, I promise to myself a better success of the second part, wherein the virtues and faults of the English poets who have written either in this, the epic, or the lyric way, will be more fully treated of, and their several styles impartially imitated.

## AN ESSAY OF DRAMATIC POESY

It was that memorable day, in the first summer of the late war, when our navy engaged the Dutch: a day wherein the two most mighty and best appointed fleets which any age had ever seen disputed the command of the greater half of the globe, the commerce of nations, and the riches of the universe. While these vast floating bodies, on either side, moved against each other in parallel lines, and our countrymen, under the happy conduct of his Royal Highness,[2] went breaking, by little and little, into the line of the enemies,

1. Dryden is probably referring particularly to the attack upon the English stage contained in Samuel Sorbière's *Relation d'un voyage en Angleterre* (1664).
2. Charles II's brother, the Duke of York, later James II.

the noise of the cannon from both navies reached our ears about the City; so that all men being alarmed with it, and in a dreadful suspense of the event which we knew was then deciding, every one went following the sound as his fancy led him; and leaving the town almost empty, some took towards the park, some cross the river, others down it; all seeking the noise in the depth of silence.

Among the rest, it was the fortune of Eugenius, Crites, Lisideius, and Neander to be in company together: three of them persons whom their wit and quality have made known to all the town, and whom I have chose to hide under these borrowed names, that they may not suffer by so ill a relation as I am going to make of their discourse.[3]

Taking then a barge which a servant of Lisideius had provided for them, they made haste to shoot the bridge, and left behind them that great fall of waters which hindered them from hearing what they desired: after which, having disengaged themselves from many vessels which rode at anchor in the Thames, and almost blocked up the passage towards Greenwich, they order the watermen to let fall their oars more gently; and then, everyone favoring his own curiosity with a strict silence, it was not long ere they perceived the air break about them like the noise of distant thunder, or of swallows in a chimney: those little undulations of sound, though almost vanishing before they reached them, yet still seeming to retain somewhat of their first horror which they had betwixt the fleets. After they had attentively listened till such time as the sound by little and little went from them, Eugenius, lifting up his head, and taking notice of it, was the first who congratulated to the rest that happy omen of our nation's victory: adding, we had but this to desire in confirmation of it, that we might hear no more of that noise which was now leaving the English coast. When the rest

3. Various attempts have been made to identify these characters, but what is relevant is an understanding of the intellectual position each of them takes: Eugenius defends the Moderns in the debate between the Ancients and the Moderns; Crites (perhaps Sir Robert Howard) defends the Ancients, and attacks rhymed dramatic verse; Lisideius (possibly an anagram of Corneille's tragedy *Le Cid*) argues for contemporary French literature; and Neander, obviously Dryden's spokesman, argues essentially for the native tradition of English drama.

had concurred in the same opinion, Crites, a person of a sharp
judgment, and somewhat too delicate a taste in wit, which the
world have mistaken in him for ill nature, said, smiling to us, that
if the concernment of this battle had not been so exceeding great,
he could scarce have wished the victory at the price he knew he
must pay for it, in being subject to the reading and hearing of so
many ill verses as he was sure would be made upon it; adding that
no argument could scape some of those eternal rhymers, who watch
a battle with more diligence than the ravens and birds of prey; and
the worst of them surest to be first in upon the quarry, while the
better able, either out of modesty writ not at all, or set that due
value upon their poems as to let them be often called for and long
expected. "There are some of those impertinent people you speak
of," answered Lisideius, "who to my knowledge are already so
provided, either way, that they can produce not only a panegyric
upon the victory but, if need be, a funeral elegy upon the Duke; and
after they have crowned his valor with many laurels, at last deplore
the odds under which he fell, concluding that his courage deserved
a better destiny." All the company smiled at the conceit[4] of Lisideius; but Crites, more eager than before, began to make particular
exceptions against some writers, and said the public magistrate
ought to send betimes to forbid them; and that it concerned the
peace and quiet of all honest people that ill poets should be as well
silenced as seditious preachers. "In my opinion," replied Eugenius,
"you pursue your point too far; for as to my own particular, I am
so great a lover of poesy that I could wish them all rewarded who
attempt but to do well; at least, I would not have them worse used
than Sylla the Dictator did one of their brethren heretofore: 'We
have seen him at a public meeting' (says Tully speaking of him),
'when a bad poet handed up from the crowd an epigram on himself,
written in rather unmetrical elegiacs. Sulla immediately ordered
him to be paid out of the proceeds of the sale, provided that he
never write again'."[5] "I could wish with all my heart," replied

4. Metaphor, image.

5. *"quem in concione vidimus cum ei libellum malus poeta de populo subjecisset, quod
epigramma in eum fecisset tantummodo alternis versibus longiusculis, statim ex iis rebus
quas tunc vendebat jubere ei præmium tribui, sub ea conditione ne quid postea scriberet"*
(Cicero, *Pro Archia poeta*, x).

Crites, "that many whom we know were as bountifully thanked upon the same condition, that they would never trouble us again. For amongst others, I have a mortal apprehension of two poets[6] whom this victory, with the help of both her wings, will never be able to escape." "'Tis easy to guess whom you intend," said Lisideius; "and without naming them, I ask you if one of them does not perpetually pay us with clenches[7] upon words and a certain clownish kind of raillery? if now and then he does not offer at a catachresis or Clevelandism,[8] wresting and torturing a word into another meaning: in fine, if he be not one of those whom the French would call *un mauvais buffon* [a bad jester]; one that is so much a well-willer to the satire that he spares no man; and though he cannot strike a blow to hurt any, yet ought to be punished for the malice of the action, as our witches are justly hanged because they think themselves so; and suffer deservedly for believing they did mischief, because they meant it." "You have described him," said Crites, "so exactly, that I am afraid to come after you with my other extremity of poetry: he is one of those who, having had some advantage of education and converse, knows better than the other what a poet should be, but puts it into practice more unluckily than any man. His style and matter are everywhere alike; he is the most calm, peaceable writer you ever read; he never disquiets your passions with the least concernment, but still leaves you in as even a temper as he found you; he is a very Leveller in poetry, he creeps along with ten little words in every line, and helps out his numbers with *for to* and *unto*, and all the pretty expletives he can find, till he drags them to the end of another line; while the sense is left tired half way behind it; he doubly starves all his verses, first for want of thought, and then of expression; his poetry neither has wit in it, nor seems to have it; like him in Martial:

Cinna wants to appear poor, and so he is.[9]

6. Probably Robert Wild and Richard Flecknoe, who actually did write wretched poems celebrating the battle.

7. Puns.

8. John Cleveland was a royalist poet whose verse represented the fag end of the metaphysical style developed by poets such as Donne and Herbert. Catachresis, or the misuse of terms, probably refers to the strain and extravagance of Cleveland's metaphors.

9. "*pauper videri Cinna vult, et est pauper*" (*Epigrams*, viii. 19).

"He affects plainness, to cover his want of imagination: when he writes the serious way, the highest flight of his fancy is some miserable antithesis, or seeming contradiction; and in the comic he is still reaching at some thin conceit, the ghost of a jest, and that too flies before him, never to be caught; these swallows which we see before us on the Thames are the just resemblance of his wit: you may observe how near the water they stoop, how many proffers they make to dip, and yet how seldom they touch it; and when they do, 'tis but the surface: they skim over it but to catch a gnat, and then mount into the air and leave it."

"Well, gentlemen," said Eugenius, "you may speak your pleasure of these authors; but though I and some few more about the town may give you a peaceable hearing, yet, assure yourselves, there are multitudes who would think you malicious and them injured: especially him whom you first described; he is the very Withers [10] of the city: they have bought more editions of his works than would serve to lay under all their pies at the Lord Mayor's Christmas. When his famous poem first came out in the year 1660, I have seen them reading it in the midst of 'Change time; nay, so vehement they were at it, that they lost their bargain by the candles' ends; [11] but what will you say if he has been received amongst the great ones? I can assure you he is, this day, the envy of a great person who is lord in the art of quibbling; and who does not take it well that any man should intrude so far into his province." "All I would wish," replied Crites, "is that they who love his writings may still admire him, and his fellow poet: 'Let him who does not hate Baevius, &c.', [12] is curse sufficient." "And farther," added Lisideius, "I believe there is no man who writes well, but would think himself very hardly dealt with, if their admirers should praise anything of his: 'For we contemn those who admire what we despise.'" [13] "There are so few who write well in this age," said Crites, "that methinks any praises should be welcome; they neither rise to the dignity of the

10. George Wither or Withers, an old Parliamentary poet, known for his doggerel verse.

11. At auctions bids were accepted as long as the candle remained burning.

12. "*qui Bavium non odit, &c*" (Virgil, *Eclogues*, III. 90). The full line reads: "Let him who does not hate Baevius love your songs, Maevius."

13. "*nam quos contemnimus, eorum quoque laudes contemnimus*" (source unknown).

last age, nor to any of the Ancients: and we may cry out of the writers of this time, with more reason than Petronius of his, 'With your permission, let me say that the rhetoricians more than anyone have been the death of eloquence':[14] you have debauched the true old poetry so far, that nature, which is the soul of it, is not in any of your writings."

"If your quarrel," said Eugenius, "to those who now write, be grounded only on your reverence to antiquity, there is no man more ready to adore those great Greeks and Romans than I am: but on the other side, I cannot think so contemptibly of the age I live in, or so dishonorably of my own country, as not to judge we equal the Ancients in most kinds of poesy, and in some surpass them; neither know I any reason why I may not be as zealous for the reputation of our age, as we find the Ancients themselves in reference to those who lived before them. For you hear your Horace saying,

I am angered when anything is condemned, not for being badly written or inelegant, but for being new.[15]

And after:

If poems improved with every passing day like wines, I should like to know which year is best for literature?[16]

"But I see I am engaging in a wide dispute, where the arguments are not like to reach close on either side; for poesy is of so large extent, and so many both of the Ancients and Moderns have done well in all kinds of it, that, in citing one against the other, we shall take up more time this evening than each man's occasions will allow him: therefore I would ask Crites to what part of poesy he would confine his arguments, and whether he would defend the general cause of the Ancients against the Moderns, or oppose any page of the Moderns against this of ours?"

14. *"pace vestra liceat dixisse, primi omnium eloquentiam perdidistis"* (*Satyricon*, 2).
15. *indignor quicquam reprehendi, non quia crasse*
   *compositum, illepidève, putetur, sed quia nuper.*
                    *Epistles*, II, i, 76–77.
16. *si meliora dies, ut vina, poemata reddit,*
   *scire velim, pretium chartis quotus arroget annus?*
                    *Ibid.*, 34–35.

Crites, a little while considering upon this demand, told Eugenius he approved his propositions and, if he pleased, he would limit their dispute to dramatic poesy; in which he thought it not difficult to prove either that the Ancients were superior to the Moderns, or the last age to this of ours.[17]

Eugenius was somewhat surprised when he heard Crites make choice of that subject. "For aught I see," said he, "I have undertaken a harder province than I imagined; for though I never judged the plays of the Greek or Roman poets comparable to ours, yet on the other side those we now see acted come short of many which were written in the last age: but my comfort is, if we are o'ercome, it will be only by our own countrymen; and if we yield to them in this one part of poesy, we more surpass them in all the other; for in the epic or lyric way it will be hard for them to show us one such amongst them, as we have many now living, or who lately were so. They can produce nothing so courtly writ, or which expresses so much the conversation of a gentleman, as Sir John Suckling; nothing so even, sweet, and flowing, as Mr. Waller; nothing so majestic, so correct, as Sir John Denham; nothing so elevated, so copious, and full of spirit, as Mr. Cowley; as for the Italian, French and Spanish plays, I can make it evident that those who now write surpass them; and that the drama is wholly ours."

All of them were thus far of Eugenius his opinion that the sweetness of English verse was never understood or practiced by our fathers; even Crites himself did not much oppose it: and every one was willing to acknowledge how much our poesy is improved by the happiness of some writers yet living, who first taught us to mould our thoughts into easy and significant words, to retrench the superfluities of expression, and to make our rhyme so properly a part of the verse, that it should never mislead the sense, but itself be led and governed by it.

Eugenius was going to continue this discourse, when Lisideius told him it was necessary, before they proceeded further, to take a

17. If Crites does represent Sir Robert Howard, then Dryden makes him argue out of character. In his preface to *Four New Plays* (1665) Howard had attacked rhyme, but he had also defended modern as opposed to classical drama.

standing measure of their controversy; for how was it possible to be decided who writ the best plays, before we know what a play should be? But, this once agreed on by both parties, each might have recourse to it, either to prove his own advantages, or discover the failings of his adversary.

He had no sooner said this, but all desired the favor of him to give the definition of a play; and they were the more importunate, because neither Aristotle, nor Horace, nor any other who writ of that subject, had ever done it.

Lisideius, after some modest denials, at last confessed he had a rude notion of it; indeed rather a description than a definition; but which served to guide him in his private thoughts, when he was to make a judgment of what others writ: that he conceived a play ought to be *A just and lively image of human nature, representing its passions and humours, and the changes of fortune to which it is subject, for the delight and instruction of mankind.*

This definition, though Crites raised a logical objection against it, that it was only *a genere et fine*,[18] and so not altogether perfect, was yet well received by the rest: and after they had given order to the watermen to turn their barge, and row softly, that they might take the cool of the evening in their return, Crites, being desired by the company to begin, spoke on behalf of the Ancients, in this manner:

"If confidence presage a victory, Eugenius, in his own opinion, has already triumphed over the Ancients: nothing seems more easy to him than to overcome those whom it is our greatest praise to have imitated well; for we do not only build upon their foundation, but by their models. Dramatic poesy had time enough, reckoning from Thespis (who first invented it) to Aristophanes, to be born, to grow up, and to flourish in maturity. It has been observed of arts and sciences, that in one and the same century they have arrived to a great perfection; and no wonder, since every age has a kind of universal genius, which inclines those that live in it to some particular studies: the work then being pushed on by many hands, must of necessity go forward.

"Is it not evident in these last hundred years (when the study of philosophy has been the business of all the virtuosi in Christendom),

18. That is, made no distinction between drama and other forms of literature.

that almost a new nature has been revealed to us? that more errors of
the school have been detected, more useful experiments in philosophy
have been made, more noble secrets in optics, medicine, anatomy,
astronomy discovered, than in all those credulous and doting ages
from Aristotle to us? so true it is that nothing spreads more fast
than science when rightly and generally cultivated.

"Add to this the more than common emulation that was in those
times of writing well; which though it be found in all ages and all
persons that pretend to the same reputation, yet poesy, being then
in more esteem than now it is, had greater honors decreed to the
professors of it, and consequently the rivalship was more high between them; they had judges ordained to decide their merit, and
prizes to reward it; and historians have been diligent to record of
Æschylus, Euripides, Sophocles, Lycophron, and the rest of them,
both who they were that vanquished in these wars of the theater,
and how often they were crowned: while the Asian kings and
Grecian commonwealths scarce afforded them a nobler subject
than the unmanly luxuries of a debauched court, or giddy intrigues
of a factious city. *Alit æmulatio ingenis* (says Paterculus), *et nunc
invidia, nunc admiratio incitationem accendit*:[19] emulation is the spur
of wit, and sometimes envy, sometimes admiration, quickens our
endeavors.

"But now, since the rewards of honor are taken away, that
virtuous emulation is turned into direct malice; yet so slothful,
that it contents itself to condemn and cry down others, without
attempting to do better: 'tis a reputation too unprofitable, to take
the necessary pains for it; yet wishing they had it is incitement
enough to hinder others from it. And this, in short, Eugenius, is
the reason why you have now so few good poets, and so many
severe judges. Certainly, to imitate the Ancients well, much labor
and long study is required; which pains, I have already shown,
our poets would want encouragement to take, if yet they had ability
to go through with it. Those Ancients have been faithful imitators
and wise observers of that nature which is so torn and ill represented in our plays; they have handed down to us a perfect resemblance of her; which we, like ill copiers, neglecting to look on, have

19. *Historia romana*, I. 17.

rendered monstrous and disfigured. But, that you may know how much you are indebted to those your masters, and be ashamed to to have so ill requited them, I must remember you that all the rules by which we practice the drama at this day, either such as relate to the justness and symmetry of the plot, or the episodical ornaments, such as descriptions, narrations, and other beauties, which are not essential to the play, were delivered to us from the observations which Aristotle made of those poets, which either lived before him, or were his contemporaries: we have added nothing of our own, except we have the confidence to say our wit is better; which none boast of in this our age, but such as understand not theirs. Of that book which Aristotle has left us, περὶ τῆς Ποιητικῆς, Horace his *Art of Poetry* is an excellent comment and, I believe, restores to us that second book of his concerning comedy, which is wanting in him.

"Out of these two has been extracted the famous rules which the French call *des trois unités*, or the Three Unities, which ought to be observed in every regular play: namely, of time, place, and action.[20]

"The unity of time they comprehend in twenty-four hours, the compass of a natural day, or as near it as can be contrived; and the reason of it is obvious to every one, that the time of the feigned action, or fable of the play, should be proportioned as near as can be to the duration of that time in which it is represented; since, therefore, all plays are acted on the theater in a space of time much within the compass of twenty-four hours, that play is to be thought the nearest imitation of nature whose plot or action is confined within that time; and, by the same rule which concludes this general proportion of time, it follows that all the parts of it are to be equally subdivided; as namely, that one act take not up the supposed time of half a day, which is out of proportion to the rest, since the other four are then to be straitened within the compass of the remaining half: for it is unnatural that one act, which

20. Crites' discussion of the three "unities" is typical of seventeenth-century distortions of Aristotle's *Poetics*. The only so-called unity Aristotle took seriously was that of action. He never suggested that constricted time or place were necessary for dramatic illusion.

being spoke or written is not longer than the rest, should be supposed longer by the audience; 'tis therefore the poet's duty to take care that no act should be imagined to exceed the time in which it is represented on the stage; and that the intervals and inequalities of time be supposed to fall out between the acts.

"This rule of time, how well it has been observed by the Ancients, most of their plays will witness; you see them in their tragedies (wherein to follow this rule is certainly most difficult) from the very beginning of their plays, falling close into that part of the story which they intend for the action or principal object of it, leaving the former part to be delivered by narration: so that they set the audience, as it were, at the post where the race is to be concluded; and, saving them the tedious expectation of seeing the poet set out and ride the beginning of the course, you behold him not till he is in sight of the goal, and just upon you.

"For the second unity, which is that of place, the Ancients meant by it that the scene ought to be continued through the play, in the same place where it was laid in the beginning: for the stage on which it is represented being but one and the same place, it is unnatural to conceive it many, and those far distant from one another. I will not deny but by the variation of painted scenes the fancy (which in these cases will contribute to its own deceit) may sometimes imagine it several places, with some appearance of probability; yet it still carries the greater likelihood of truth if those places be supposed so near each other, as in the same town or city; which may all be comprehended under the larger denomination of one place: for a greater distance will bear no proportion to the shortness of time which is allotted in the acting, to pass from one of them to another; for the observation of this, next to the Ancients, the French are to be most commended. They tie themselves so strictly to the unity of place that you never see in any of their plays a scene changed in the middle of an act: if the act begins in a garden, a street, or chamber, 'tis ended in the same place; and that you may know it to be the same, the stage is so supplied with persons that it is never empty all the time: he that enters the second has business with him who was on before; and before the second quits the stage, a third appears who has business with him. This Corneille calls *la liaison des scènes*, the continuity or joining of the scenes; and 'tis a good mark of a well contrived play when all the persons are known to each other, and every one of them has some affairs with all the rest.

"As for the third unity, which is that of action, the Ancients meant no other by it than what the logicians do by their *finis*, the end or scope of any action; that which is the first in intention, and last in execution: now the poet is to aim at one great and complete action, to the carrying on of which all things in his play, even the very obstacles, are to be subservient; and the reason of this is as evident as any of the former.

"For two actions, equally labored and driven on by the writer, would destroy the unity of the poem; it would be no longer one play, but two: not but that there may be many actions in a play, as Ben Jonson has observed in his *Discoveries*; but they must be all subservient to the great one, which our language happily expresses in the name of *under-plots*: such as in Terence's *Eunuch* is the difference and reconcilement of Thais and Phaedria, which is not the chief business of the play, but promotes the marriage of Chaerea and Chremes's sister, principally intended by the poet. There ought to be but one action, says Corneille, that is, one complete action which leaves the mind of the audience in a full repose: but this cannot be brought to pass but by many other imperfect ones which conduce to it, and hold the audience in a delightful suspense of what will be.[21]

"If by these rules (to omit many other drawn from the precepts and practice of the Ancients) we should judge our modern plays, 'tis probable that few of them would endure the trial: that which should be the business of a day, takes up in some of them an age; instead of one action, they are the epitomes of a man's life; and for one spot of ground (which the stage should represent) we are sometimes in more countries than the map can show us.

"But if we will allow the Ancients to have contrived well, we must acknowledge them to have writ better; questionless we are deprived of a great stock of wit in the loss of Menander among the

21. Dryden translates Corneille verbatim: "*Il n'y doit avoir qu'une action complète, qui laisse l'esprit de l'auditeur dans le calme; mais elle ne peut le devenir que par plusieurs autres imparfaites qui lui servent d'acheminements, et tiennent cet auditeur dans une agréable suspension*" (*Discours des trois unités*).

Greek poets, and of Caecilius, Afranus, and Varius among the Romans; we may guess of Menander's excellency by the plays of Terence, who translated some of his, and yet wanted so much of him that he was called by C. Caesar the half-Menander; and of Varius, by the testimonies of Horace, Martial, and Velleius Paterculus. 'Tis probable that these, could they be recovered, would decide the controversy; but so long as Aristophanes in the old comedy and Plautus in the new are extant, while the tragedies of Euripides, Sophocles, and Seneca, are to be had, I can never see one of those plays which are now written but it increases my admiration of the Ancients; and yet I must acknowledge further that, to admire them as we ought, we should understand them better than we do. Doubtless many things appear flat to us, whose wit depended on some custom or story which never came to our knowledge; or perhaps upon some criticism in their language, which being so long dead, and only remaining in their books, 'tis not possible they should make us know it perfectly. To read Macrobius explaining the propriety and elegancy of many words in Virgil which I had before passed over without consideration as common things, is enough to assure me that I ought to think the same of Terence; and that in the purity of his style (which Tully so much valued that he ever carried his works about him) there is yet left in him great room for admiration, if I knew but where to place it. In the meantime I must desire you to take notice that the greatest man of the last age (Ben Jonson) was willing to give place to them in all things: he was not only a professed imitator of Horace, but a learned plagiary of all the others; you track him everywhere in their snow: if Horace, Lucan, Petronius Arbiter, Seneca, and Juvenal had their own from him, there are few serious thoughts which are new in him: you will pardon me, therefore, if I presume he loved their fashion, when he wore their clothes. But since I have otherwise a great veneration for him, and you, Eugenius, prefer him above all other poets, I will use no farther argument to you than his example: I will produce Father Ben to you, dressed in all the ornaments and colors of the Ancients; you will need no other guide to our party if you follow him; and whether you consider the bad plays of our age, or regard the good ones of the last, both the best and worst of the modern poets will equally instruct you to esteem the Ancients."

Crites had no sooner left speaking, but Eugenius, who waited with some impatience for it, thus began:

"I have observed in your speech that the former part of it is convincing as to what the Moderns have profited by the rules of the Ancients; but in the latter you are careful to conceal how much they have excelled them. We own all the helps we have from them, and want neither veneration nor gratitude while we acknowledge that to overcome them we must make use of the advantages we have received from them: but to these assistances we have joined our own industry; for (had we sat down with a dull imitation of them) we might then have lost somewhat of the old perfection, but never acquired any that was new. We draw not therefore after their lines, but those of nature; and having the life before us, besides the experience of all they knew, it is no wonder if we hit some airs and features which they have missed. I deny not what you urge of arts and sciences, that they have flourished in some ages more than others; but your instance in philosophy makes for me: for if natural causes be more known now than in the time of Aristotle, because more studied, it follows that poesy and other arts may with the same pains arrive still nearer to perfection; and, that granted, it will rest for you to prove that they wrought more perfect images of human life than we; which, seeing in your discourse you have avoided to make good, it shall now be my task to show you some part of their defects, and some few excellencies of the Moderns. And I think there is none among us can imagine I do it enviously, or with purpose to detract from them; for what interest of fame or profit can the living lose by the reputation of the dead? On the other side, it is a great truth which Velleius Paterculus affirms: 'We are more disposed to praise what we have heard than what we have seen; the present we regard with envy, the past with admiration, and we believe ourselves obscured by the one while we learn from the other':22 that praise or censure is certainly the most sincere which unbribed posterity shall give us.

22. "*audita visis libentius laudamus; et præsentia invidia, præterita admiratione prose-quimir; et his nos obrui, illis instrui credimus*" (*Historia romana*, II. 92).

"Be pleased then in the first place to take notice that the Greek poesy, which Crites has affirmed to have arrived to perfection in the reign of the Old Comedy, was so far from it that the distinction of it into acts was not known to them; or if it were, it is yet so darkly delivered to us that we cannot make it out.

"All we know of it is from the singing of their Chorus, and that too is so uncertain that in some of their plays we have reason to conjecture they sung more than five times. Aristotle indeed divides the integral parts of a play into four.[23] First, the *protasis*, or entrance, which gives light only to the characters of the persons, and proceeds very little into any part of the action. Secondly, the *epitasis*, or working up of the plot, where the play grows warmer, the design or action of it is drawing on, and you see something promising that it will come to pass. Thirdly, the *catastasis*, or counterturn, which destroys that expectation, imbroils the action in new difficulties, and leaves you far distant from that hope in which it found you; as you may have observed in a violent stream resisted by a narrow passage: it runs round to an eddy, and carries back the waters with more swiftness than it brought them on. Lastly, the *catastrophe*, which the Grecians called λύσις, the French *le dénouement*, and we the discovery or unravelling of the plot; there you see all things settling again upon their first foundations, and the obstacles which hindered the design or action of the play once removed, it ends with that resemblance of truth and nature that the audience are satisfied with the conduct of it. Thus this great man delivered to us the image of a play, and I must confess it is so lively that from thence much light has been derived to the forming it more perfectly into acts and scenes; but what poet first limited to five the number of the acts, I know not, only we see it so firmly established in the time of Horace that he gives it for a rule in comedy: 'Let no play be shorter or longer than five acts.'[24] So that you see the Grecians cannot be said to have consummated this art; writing rather by entrances than by acts, and having rather a general indigested

23. The four parts were enumerated by the Italian Renaissance critic J. C. Scaliger, not Aristotle.
24. "*neu brevior quinto, neu sit productior actu*" (misquoted from *Ars Poetica*, l. 189).

notion of a play, than knowing how and where to bestow the particular graces of it.

"But since the Spaniards at this day allow but three acts, which they call *jornadas*, to a play, and the Italians in many of theirs follow them, when I condemn the Ancients, I declare it is not altogether because they have not five acts to every play, but because they have not confined themselves to one certain number: 'tis building an house without a model; and when they succeeded in such undertakings, they ought to have sacrificed to Fortune, not to the Muses.

"Next, for the plot, which Aristotle called 'the fable,' and often 'the arrangement of events,'[25] and from him the Romans *fabula*, it has already been judiciously observed by a late writer[26] that in their tragedies it was only some tale derived from Thebes or Troy, or at least something that happened in those two ages, which was worn so threadbare by the pens of all the epic poets, and even by tradition itself of the talkative Greeklings (as Ben Jonson calls them) that before it came upon the stage it was already known to all the audience: and the people, so soon as ever they heard the name of Oedipus, knew as well as the poet that he had killed his father by a mistake, and committed incest with his mother, before the play; that they were now to hear of a great plague, an oracle, and the ghost of Laius: so that they sat with a yawning kind of expectation, till he was to come with his eyes pulled out, and speak a hundred or two of verses in a tragic tone, in complaint of his misfortunes. But one Oedipus, Hercules, or Medea had been tolerable: poor people, they scaped not so good cheap; they had still the *chapon bouillé* [boiled capon] set before them, till their appetites were cloyed with the same dish, and the novelty being gone, the pleasure vanished; so that one main end of dramatic poesy in its definition, which was to cause delight, was of consequence destroyed.

"In their comedies, the Romans generally borrowed their plots from the Greek poets; and theirs was commonly a little girl stolen

25. "τὸ μῦθος, . . . τῶε πραγμάτων σύνθεσις."
26. Sir Robert Howard, in his preface to *Four New Plays* (1665).

or wandered from her parents, brought back unknown to the same city, there got with child by some lewd young fellow who, by the help of his servant, cheats his father; and when her time comes to cry 'Mother Juno, do your job'[27] one or other sees a little box or cabinet which was carried away with her, and so discovers her to her friends, if some god do not prevent it by coming down in a machine, and take the thanks of it to himself.

"By the plot you may guess much of the characters of the persons. An old father who would willingly, before he dies, see his son well married; his debauched son, kind in his nature to his wench, but miserably in want of money; a servant or slave, who has so much wit to strike in with him, and help to dupe his father; a braggadocio captain, a parasite, and a lady of pleasure.

"As for the poor honest maid, whom all the story is built upon, and who ought to be one of the principal actors in the play, she is commonly a mute in it: she has the breeding of the old Elizabeth way, for maids to be seen and not to be heard; and it is enough you know she is willing to be married when the fifth act requires it.

"These are plots built after the Italian mode of houses: you see through them all at once. The characters are indeed the imitations of nature, but so narrow as if they had imitated only an eye or an hand, and did not dare to venture on the lines of a face, or the proportion of a body.

"But in how strait a compass soever they have bounded their plots and characters, we will pass it by if they have regularly pursued them, and perfectly observed those three unities of time, place, and action; the knowledge of which you say is derived to us from them. But in the first place give me leave to tell you that the unity of place, however it might be practiced by them, was never any of their rules: we neither find it in Aristotle, Horace, or any who have written of it, till in our age the French poets first made it a precept of the stage.[28] The unity of time even Terence himself (who was the best and most regular of them) has neglected: his *Heautontimorumenos*, or *Self-Punisher*, takes up visibly two days;

27. "*Juno Lucina, fer opem*" (Terence, *Andria*, III. i. 15).
28. The rule was actually promulgated by the Italian critic Castelvetro.

therefore, says Scaliger, the two first acts concluding the first day were acted overnight; the three last on the ensuing day; and Euripides, in tying himself to one day, has committed an absurdity never to be forgiven him; for in one of his tragedies he has made Theseus go from Athens to Thebes, which was about forty English miles, under the walls of it to give battle, and appear victorious in the next act; and yet, from the time of his departure to the return of the Nuntius, who gives the relation of his victory, Æthra and the Chorus have but thirty-six verses; that is not for every mile a verse.[29]

"The like error is as evident in Terence his *Eunuch*, when Laches, the old man, enters in a mistake the house of Thais; where, betwixt his exit and the entrance of Pythias, who comes to give an ample relation of the garboiles he has raised within, Parmeno, who was left upon the stage, has not above five lines to speak. 'This is a fine use of so short a time,' says the French poet who furnished me with one of the observations;[30] and almost all their tragedies will afford us examples of the like nature.

"'Tis true, they have kept the continuity or, as you called it, *liaison des scènes*, somewhat better: two do not perpetually come in together, talk, and go out together; and other two succeed them, and do the same throughout the act, which the English call by the name of single scenes; but the reason is, because they have seldom above two or three scenes, properly so called, in every act; for it is to be accounted a new scene, not every time the stage is empty, but every person who enters, though to others, makes it so; because he introduces a new business. Now the plots of their plays being narrow, and the persons few, one of their acts was written in a less compass than one of our well wrought scenes; and yet they are often deficient even in this. To go no further than Terence, you find in the *Eunuch* Antipho entering single in the midst of the third act, after Chremes and Pythias were gone off;[31] in the same play you have likewise Dorias beginning the fourth act alone; and after

29. This paragraph is substantially indebted to Corneille's third *Discours*.
30. "*C'est bien employ[er] un temps si court.*" The French poet is Corneille.
31. Also based on Corneille's third *Discours*.

she has made a relation of what was done at the soldier's entertainment (which by the way was very inartificial [32] to do, because
she was presumed to speak directly to the audience, and to acquaint
them with what was necessary to be known, but yet should have been
so contrived by the poet as to have been told by persons of the drama
to one another, and so by them to have come to the knowledge of
the people), she quits the stage, and Phaedria enters next, alone
likewise: he also gives you an account of himself, and of his returning
from the country, in monologue; to which unnatural way of narration Terence is subject in all his plays. In his *Adelphi*, or *Brothers*,
Syrus and Demea enter after the scene was broken by the departure
of Sostrata, Geta, and Canthara; and indeed you can scarce look
into any of his comedies, where you will not presently discover the
same interruption.

"But as they have failed both in laying of their plots, and managing of them, swerving from the rules of their own art by misrepre-
senting nature to us, in which they have ill satisfied one intention
of a play, which was delight; so in the instructive part they have
erred worse: instead of punishing vice and rewarding virtue, they
have often shown a prosperous wickedness, and an unhappy piety:
they have set before us a bloody image of revenge in Medea, and
given her dragons to convey her safe from punishment; a Priam
and Astyanax murdered, and Cassandra ravished, and the lust and
murder ending in the victory of him that acted them: in short,
there is no indecorum in any of our modern plays which, if I would
excuse, I could not shadow with some authority from the Ancients.

"And one farther note of them let me leave you: tragedies and
comedies were not writ then as they are now, promiscuously, by
the same person; but he who found his genius bending to the one,
never attempted the other way. This is so plain, that I need not
instance to you that Aristophanes, Plautus, Terence, never any
of them writ a tragedy; Æschylus, Euripides, Sophocles, and
Seneca never meddled with comedy: the sock and buskin were not
worn by the same poet. Having then so much care to excel in one
kind, very little is to be pardoned them if they miscarried in it;
and this would lead me to the consideration of their wit, had not

32. Inartistic. "Artifice" and "artificial" are terms of praise in Restoration
criticism.

Crites given me sufficient warning not to be too bold in my judgment of it; because the languages being dead, and many of the customs and little accidents on which it depended lost to us, we are not competent judges of it. But though I grant that here and there we may miss the application of a proverb or a custom, yet a thing well said will be wit in all languages; and though it may lose something in the translation, yet to him who reads it in the original, 'tis still the same: he has an idea of its excellency, though it cannot pass from his mind into any other expression or words than those in which he finds it. When Phaedria, in the *Eunuch*, had a command from his mistress to be absent two days, and, encouraging himself to go through with it, said, 'But am I to do without her, if I have to, for all of three days?'[33]—Parmeno, to mock the softness of his master, lifting up his hands and eyes, cries out, as it were in admiration, *hui! universum triduum!* the elegancy of which *universum*, though it cannot be rendered in our language, yet leaves an impression of the wit upon our souls: but this happens seldom in him; in Plautus oftener, who is infinitely too bold in his metaphors and coining words, out of which many times his wit is nothing; which questionless was one reason why Horace falls upon him so severely in those verses:

> Yet our fathers lauded Plautus's verse and his wit, being too patient, not to say stupid.[34]

For Horace himself was cautious to obtrude a new word upon his readers, and makes custom and common use the best measure of receiving it into our writings:

> Many terms fallen out of use shall be reborn, and others now honored shall fall, if usage wills it so, in whose power lies the standard and the law and the rule of speech.[35]

---

33. *"tandem ego non illa caream, si sit opus, vel totum triduum?"* (*Eunuch*, II. i. 17–18). Parmeno answers, "Three *whole* days!"

34. *sed proavi nostri Plautinos et numeros et*
   *laudavere sales, nimium patienter utrumque,*
   *ne dicam stolidè.*
         *Ars poetica*, ll. 270–272.

35. *multa renascentur quae nunc cecidere, cadentque*
   *quae nunc sunt in honore vocabula, si volet usus,*
   *quem penes arbitrium est, et jus, et norma loquendi.*
         *Ibid.*, ll. 70–72.

"The not observing this rule is that which the world has blamed in our satirist, Cleveland: to express a thing hard and unnaturally, is his new way of elocution. 'Tis true, no poet but may sometimes use a catachresis; Virgil does it:

> . . . shall pour forth the Egyptian bean blended with the smiling acanthus,[36]

in his eclogue of Pollio; and in his 7th Æneid,

> The very waves and unaccustomed woods admire the warriors' shining shields and the painted hulls.[37]

And Ovid once so modestly, that he asks leave to do it:

> If I may be so audacious as to say it, I would not fear to call it the Palatia of heaven itself,[38]

calling the court of Jupiter by the name of Augustus his palace, though in another place he is more bold, where he says, 'and Capitols view long processions.'[39] But to do this always, and never be able to write a line without it, though it may be admired by some few pedants, will not pass upon those who know that wit is best conveyed to us in the most easy language; and is most to be admired when a great thought comes dressed in words so commonly received that it is understood by the meanest apprehensions, as the best meat is the most easily digested: but we cannot read a verse of Cleveland's without making a face at it, as if every word were a pill to swallow: he gives us many times a hard nut to break our teeth, without a kernel for our pains. So that there is this difference betwixt his satires and Doctor Donne's, that the one gives us deep thoughts in common language, though rough cadence; the other gives us common thoughts in abstruse words. 'Tis true, in some

---

36. *"mixtaque ridenti colocasia fundet acantho"* (*Eclogues*, IV, 20).
37. . . . *mirantur et undae,*
     *miratur nemus insuetum fulgentia longe*
     *scuta virum fluvio pictasque innare carinas.*
                         *Aeneid,* VIII, 91–93.
38. . . . *si verbo audacia detur,*
     *haud metuam summi dixisse Palatia caeli.*
                         *Metamorphoses,* I, 175–176.
39. *"et longas visent Capitolia pompas"* (*Ibid.*, I, 561).

places his wit is independent of his words, as in that of the *Rebel Scot*:

> Had *Cain* been *Scot*, God would have chang'd his doom;
> Not forc'd him wander, but confin'd him home.

"'If only he had always spoken so!'[40] This is wit in all languages: 'tis like mercury, never to be lost or killed: and so that other:

> For beauty like white-powder makes no noise,
> And yet the silent hypocrite destroys.[41]

You see, the last line is highly metaphorical, but it is so soft and gentle that it does not shock us as we read it.

"But, to return from whence I have digressed to the consideration of the Ancients' writing and their wit (of which by this time you will grant us in some measure to be fit judges). Though I see many excellent thoughts in Seneca, yet he of them who had genius most proper for the stage was Ovid; he had a way of writing so fit to stir up a pleasing admiration and concernment, which are the objects of a tragedy, and to show the various movements of a soul combating betwixt two different passions that, had he lived in our age, or in his own could have writ with our advantages, no man but must have yielded to him; and therefore I am confident the *Medea* is none of his: for though I esteem it for the gravity and sententiousness of it, which he himself concludes to be suitable to a tragedy, 'tragedy surpasses all other kinds of writing in gravity,'[42] yet it moves not my soul enough to judge that he who in the epic way wrote things so near the drama as the story of Myrrha, of Caunus and Biblis, and the rest, should stir up no more concernment where he most endeavored it. The master-piece of Seneca I hold to be that scene in the *Troades* where Ulysses is seeking for Astyanax to kill him; there you see the tenderness of a mother so represented in Andromache that it raises compassion to a high degree in the reader, and bears the nearest resemblance of any thing in their

40. "*Si sic omnia dixisset!*" (Juvenal, *Satires*, X. 123–124). The couplet Dryden cites from Cleveland is from "Rebel Scot," ll. 63–64.

41. Cleveland, "Rupertismus," ll. 39–40. The "white-powder" is a supposed kind of gunpowder, exploding without noise.

42. "*omne genus scripti gravitate tragædia vincit*" (*Tristia*, II. 381).

tragedies to the excellent scenes of passion in Shakespeare, or in
Fletcher: for love-scenes, you will find few among them, their
tragic poets dealt not with that soft passion but with lust, cruelty,
revenge, ambition, and those bloody actions they produced; which
were more capable of raising horror than compassion in an
audience: leaving love untouched, whose gentleness would have
tempered them, which is the most frequent of all the passions,
and which, being the private concernment of every person, is
soothed by viewing its own image in a public entertainment.

"Among their comedies, we find a scene or two of tenderness,
and that where you would least expect it, in Plautus; but to speak
generally, their lovers say little, when they see each other, but
'my soul, my life; my life and soul,'[43] as the women in Juvenal's
time used to cry out in the fury of their kindness: then indeed to
speak sense were an offense. Any sudden gust of passion (as an
ecstasy of love in an unexpected meeting) cannot better be expressed
than in a word and a sigh, breaking one another. Nature is dumb on
such occasions, and to make her speak would be to represent her
unlike herself. But there are a thousand other concernments of
lovers, as jealousies, complaints, contrivances, and the like, where not
to open their minds at large to each other were to be wanting
to their own love, and to the expectation of the audience; who
watch the movements of their minds, as much as the changes of
their fortunes. For the imaging of the first is properly the work
of a poet; the latter he borrows of the historian."

Eugenius was proceeding in that part of his discourse, when
Crites interrupted him. "I see," said he, "Eugenius and I are never
like to have this question decided betwixt us; for he maintains the
Moderns have acquired a new perfection in writing, I can only
grant they have altered the mode of it. Homer described his heroes
men of great appetites, lovers of beef broiled upon the coals, and
good fellows; contrary to the practice of the French romances,
whose heroes neither eat, nor drink, nor sleep, for love. Virgil makes
Æneas a bold avower of his own virtues:

> I am the dutiful Aeneas, famed through report
> throughout the world;[44]

43. *"anima mea, vita mea; ζωὴ καὶ ψυχη."*
44. *"sum pius Æneas, fama super æthera notus"* (*Aeneid*, I. 378–379).

which in the civility of our poets is the character of a Fanfaron or Hector: for with us the knight takes occasion to walk out, or sleep, to avoid the vanity of telling his own story, which the trusty squire is ever to perform for him. So in their love-scenes, of which Eugenius spoke last, the Ancients were more hearty, we more talkative: they writ love as it was then the mode to make it; and I will grant thus much to Eugenius, that perhaps one of their poets, had he lived in our age,

if fate had postponed his birth to this age of ours [45]

(as Horace says of Lucilius), he had altered many things; not that they were not as natural before, but that he might accommodate himself to the age he lived in. Yet in the meantime, we are not to conclude any thing rashly against those great men, but preserve to them the dignity of masters, and give that honor to their memories ('whom the funeral goddess has consecrated') [46] part of which we expect may be paid to us in future times."

This moderation of Crites, as it was pleasing to all the company, so it put an end to that dispute; which Eugenius, who seemed to have the better of the argument, would urge no farther: but Lisideius, after he had acknowledged himself of Eugenius his opinion concerning the Ancients, yet told him he had forborne, till his discourse were ended, to ask him why he preferred the English plays above those of other nations? and whether we ought not to submit our stage to the exactness of our next neighbors?

"Though," said Eugenius, "I am at all times ready to defend the honor of my country against the French, and to maintain we are as well able to vanquish them with our pens as our ancestors have been with their swords; yet, if you please," added he, looking upon Neander, "I will commit this cause to my friend's management; his opinion of our plays is the same with mine: and besides, there is no reason that Crites and I, who have now left the stage, should re-enter so suddenly upon it; which is against the laws of comedy."

"If the question had been stated," replied Lisideius, "who had writ best, the French or English, forty years ago, I should have

45. *"si foret hoc nostrum fato delapsus in ævum"* (*Satires*, I. 10. 68).
46. *"quos Libitina sacravit"* (Horace, *Epistles*, II. i. 49).

been of your opinion, and adjudged the honor to our own nation; but since that time," said he (turning towards Neander), "we have been so long together bad Englishmen, that we had not leisure to be good poets. Beaumont, Fletcher, and Jonson (who were only capable of bringing us to that degree of perfection which we have) were just then leaving the world, as if, in an age of so much horror, wit and those milder studies of humanity had no farther business among us. But the Muses, who ever follow peace, went to plant in another country: it was then that the great Cardinal of Richelieu began to take them into his protection; and that, by his encouragement, Corneille and some other Frenchmen reformed their theater, which before was as much below ours, as it now surpasses it and the rest of Europe. But because Crites in his discourse for the Ancients has prevented me, by touching upon many rules of the stage which the Moderns have borrowed from them, I shall only, in short, demand of you whether you are not convinced that of all nations the French have best observed them? In the unity of time you find them so scrupulous that it yet remains a dispute among their poets whether the artificial day of twelve hours, more or less, be not meant by Aristotle, rather than the natural one of twenty-four; and consequently whether all plays ought not to be reduced into that compass. This I can testify, that in all their dramas writ within these last twenty years and upwards, I have not observed any that have extended the time to thirty hours. In the unity of place they are full as scrupulous, for many of their critics limit it to that very spot of ground where the play is supposed to begin; none of them exceed the compass of the same town or city.

"The unity of action in all plays is yet more conspicuous, for they do not burden them with under-plots, as the English do; which is the reason why many scenes of our tragi-comedies carry on a design that is nothing of kin to the main plot; and that we see two distinct webs in a play, like those in ill wrought stuffs; and two actions, that is, two plays, carried on together, to the confounding of the audience; who, before they are warm in their concernments for one part, are diverted to another; and by that means espouse the interest of neither. From hence likewise it arises that the one half of our actors are not known to the other. They keep their distances, as if they were Montagues and Capulets, and seldom begin an acquaintance till the last scene of the fifth act, when they are all to meet upon the stage. There is no theater in the world has any thing so absurd as the English tragi-comedy; 'tis a drama of our own invention, and the fashion of it is enough to proclaim it so; here a course of mirth, there another of sadness and passion, a third of honor, and fourth a duel: thus, in two hours and a half we run through all the fits of Bedlam. The French affords you as much variety on the same day, but they do it not so unseasonably, or *mal à propos*, as we: our poets present you the play and the farce together; and our stages still retain somewhat of the original civility of the Red Bull.[47]

> And the groundlings are capable, in the midst of a play, of demanding
> a boxing match or a bear fight.[48]

"The end of tragedies or serious plays, says Aristotle, is to beget admiration, compassion, or concernment; but are not mirth and compassion things incompatible? and is it not evident that the poet must of necessity destroy the former by intermingling of the latter? that is, he must ruin the sole end and object of his tragedy to introduce somewhat that is forced in, and is not of the body of it. Would you not think that physician mad who, having pre-scribed a purge, should immediately order you to take restringents upon it?

"But to leave our plays, and return to theirs, I have noted one great advantage they have had in the plotting of their tragedies: that is, they are always grounded upon some known history; according to that of Horace, 'from the familiar I shall create poetry';[49] and in that they have so imitated the Ancients that they have surpassed them. For the Ancients, as was observed before,

47. An open-air theater in London, built in the early seventeenth century, and known for extravagant and melodramatic productions as well as bearbaiting.

48. "*atque ursum et pugiles media inter carmina poscunt*" (Horace, *Epistles*, II. i. 185–186).

49. "*ex noto fictum carmen sequar*" (*Ars poetica*, l. 240).

took for the foundation of their plays some poetical fiction such as under that consideration could move but little concernment in the audience, because they already knew the event of it. But the French goes farther:

> and so Homer feigns, so mingling the false with the true that the middle is never out of tune with the beginning, nor the end with the middle.[50]

He so interweaves truth with probable fiction, that he puts a pleasing fallacy upon us; mends the intrigues of fate, and dispenses with the severity of history, to reward that virtue which has been rendered to us there unfortunate. Sometimes the story has left the success so doubtful, that the writer is free, by the privilege of a poet, to take that which of two or more relations will best suit with his design: as, for example, the death of Cyrus, whom Justin and some others report to have perished in the Scythian war, but Xenophon affirms to have died in his bed of extreme old age. Nay more, when the event is past dispute, even then we are willing to be deceived, and the poet, if he contrives it with appearance of truth, has all the audience of his party; at least during the time his play is acting: so naturally we are kind to virtue, when our own interest is not in question, that we take it up as the general concernment of mankind. On the other side, if you consider the historical plays of Shakespeare, they are rather so many chronicles of kings, or the business many times of thirty or forty years, cramped into a representation of two hours and an half, which is not to imitate or paint nature, but rather to draw her in miniature, to take her in little; to look upon her through the wrong end of a perspective,[51] and receive her images not only much less, but infinitely more imperfect than the life: this, instead of making a play delightful, renders it ridiculous.

Whatever you show me in this way, I dislike and do not believe.[52]

50. *atque ita mentitur, sic veris falsa remiscet,*
　　*primo ne medium, medio ne discrepet imum.*
　　　　　　　*Ibid.*, 151–152.
51. A telescope.
52. "*quodcumque ostendis mihi sic, incredulus odi*" (Horace, *Ars poetica*, l. 188).

For the spirit of man cannot be satisfied but with truth, or at least verisimility; and a poem is to contain, if not 'the truth,' yet 'the likeness of truth,'[53] as one of the Greek poets has expressed it.

"Another thing in which the French differ from us and from the Spaniards is that they do not embarrass or cumber themselves with too much plot; they only represent so much of a story as will constitute one whole and great action sufficient for a play; we, who undertake more, do but multiply adventures; which, not being produced from one another, as effects from causes, but barely following, constitute many actions in the drama, and consequently make it many plays.

"But by pursuing close one argument, which is not cloyed with many turns, the French have gained more liberty for verse, in which they write; they have leisure to dwell on a subject which deserves it; and to represent the passions (which we have acknowledged to be the poet's work), without being hurried from one thing to another, as we are in the plays of Calderón, which we have seen lately upon our theaters under the name of Spanish plots. I have taken notice but of one tragedy of ours, whose plot has that uniformity and unity of design in it which I have commended in the French; and that is Rollo,[54] or rather, under the name of Rollo, the story of Bassianus and Geta in Herodian: there indeed the plot is neither large nor intricate, but just enough to fill the minds of the audience, not to cloy them. Besides, you see it founded upon the truth of history, only the time of the action is not reduceable to the strictness of the rules; and you see in some places a little farce mingled, which is below the dignity of the other parts; and in this all our poets are extremely peccant. Even Ben Jonson himself in Sejanus and Catiline has given us this oleo of a play, this unnatural mixture of comedy and tragedy, which to me sounds just as ridiculously as the history of David with the merry humours of Golias. In Sejanus you may take notice of the scene betwixt Livia and the physician, which is a pleasant satire upon the artificial helps of beauty; in Catiline you may see the parliament of women, the little

53. "τὰ ἔτυμα . . . ἐτύμοισιν ὁμοῖα" (Hesiod, Theogony, l. 27).

54. Rollo, or The Bloody Brother (first published 1639), by John Fletcher and others.

envies of them to one another; and all that passes betwixt Curio and Fulvia: scenes admirable in their kind, but of an ill mingle with the rest.

"But I return again to the French writers who, as I have said, do not burden themselves too much with plot, which has been reproached to them by an ingenious person of our nation[55] as a fault, for he says they commonly make but one person considerable in a play; they dwell upon him, and his concernments, while the rest of the persons are only subservient to set him off. If he intends this by it, that there is one person in the play who is of greater dignity than the rest, he must tax not only theirs, but those of the Ancients, and which he would be loth to do, the best of ours; for 'tis impossible but that one person must be more conspicuous in it than any other, and consequently the greatest share in the action must devolve on him. We see it so in the management of all affairs; even in the most equal aristocracy, the balance cannot be so justly poised but some one will be superior to the rest, either in parts, fortune, interest, or the consideration of some glorious exploit; which will reduce the greatest part of business into his hands.

"But if he would have us to imagine that in exalting of one character the rest of them are neglected, and that all of them have not some share or other in the action of the play, I desire him to produce any of Corneille's tragedies, wherein every person (like so many servants in a well governed family) has not some employment, and who is not necessary to the carrying on of the plot, or at least to your understanding it.

"There are indeed some protatic persons[56] in the Ancients, whom they make use of in their plays, either to hear or give the relation: but the French avoid this with great address, making their narrations only to, or by, such who are some way interested in the main design. And now I am speaking of relations, I cannot take a fitter opportunity to add this in favor of the French, that they often

55. Thomas Sprat, a historian of the Royal Society, author of the answer to Sorbière's attack upon the English stage entitled *Observations on Monsieur de Sorbier's Voyage into England* (1665). See headnote, above.

56. Characters pertaining to the *protasis* of the play, i.e., characters employed solely for the purposes of exposition.

use them with better judgment and more *à propos* than the English do. Not that I commend narrations in general, but there are two sorts of them: one, of those things which are antecedent to the play, and are related to make the conduct of it more clear to us; but 'tis a fault to choose such subjects for the stage which will inforce us upon that rock, because we see they are seldom listened to by the audience, and that is many times the ruin of the play. For, being once let pass without attention, the audience can never recover themselves to understand the plot; and indeed it is somewhat unreasonable that they should be put to so much trouble as, that to comprehend what passes in their sight, they must have recourse to what was done, perhaps, ten or twenty years ago.

"But there is another sort of relations, that is, of things happening in the action of the play, and supposed to be done behind the scenes; and this is many times both convenient and beautiful; for by it the French avoid the tumult which we are subject to in England by representing duels, battles, and the like, which renders our stage too like the theaters where they fight prizes. For what is more ridiculous than to represent an army with a drum and five men behind it, all which the hero of the other side is to drive in before him; or to see a duel fought, and one slain with two or three thrusts of the foils, which we know are so blunted that we might give a man an hour to kill another in good earnest with them.

"I have observed that in all our tragedies the audience cannot forbear laughing when the actors are to die; 'tis the most comic part of the whole play. All *passions* may be lively represented on the stage, if to the well-writing of them the actor supplies a good commanded voice, and limbs that move easily, and without stiffness; but there are many *actions* which can never be imitated to a just height: dying especially is a thing which none but a Roman gladiator could naturally perform on the stage, when he did not imitate or represent, but naturally do it; and therefore it is better to omit the representation of it.

"The words of a good writer, which describe it lively, will make a deeper impression of belief in us than all the actor can persuade us to when he seems to fall dead before us; as a poet in the description of a beautiful garden, or a meadow, will please our imagination

more than the place itself can please our sight. When we see death
represented, we are convinced it is but fiction; but when we hear it
related, our eyes (the strongest witnesses) are wanting, which might
have undeceived us, and we are all willing to favor the sleight when
the poet does not too grossly impose upon us. They, therefore, who
imagine these relations would make no concernment in the audience,
are deceived by confounding them with the other, which are of
things antecedent to the play: those are made often in cold blood
(as I may say) to the audience; but these are warmed with our
concernments, which are before awakened in the play. What the
philosophers say of motion, that when it is once begun it continues
of itself, and will do so to eternity without some stop put to it, is
clearly true on this occasion: the soul, being already moved with the
characters and fortunes of those imaginary persons, continues
going of its own accord; and we are no more weary to hear what
becomes of them when they are not on the stage than we are to
listen to the news of an absent mistress. But it is objected that if one
part of the play may be related, then why not all? I answer, some
parts of the action are more fit to be represented, some to be related.
Corneille says judiciously that the poet is not obliged to expose
to view all particular actions which conduce to the principal: he
ought to select such of them to be seen which will appear with the
greatest beauty, either by the magnificence of the show, or the
vehemence of passions which they produce, or some other charm
which they have in them, and let the rest arrive to the audience by
narration.[57] 'Tis a great mistake in us to believe the French present
no part of the action on the stage: every alteration or crossing of a
design, every new-sprung passion, and turn of it, is a part of the
action, and much the noblest, except we conceive nothing to be
action till they come to blows; as if the painting of the hero's mind
were not more properly the poet's work than the strength of his

---

57. Dryden is translating from Corneille's *Discours des trois unités*: "*Le poète
n'est pas tenu d'exposer à la vue toutes les actions particulières qui amènent à la principale:
il doit choisir celles qui lui sont le plus advantageuses à faire voir, soit par la beauté du
spectacle, soit par l'éclat et la véhémence des passions qu'elles produisent, soit par quelque
autre agrément qui leur soit attaché, et cacher les autres derrière la scène, pour les faire
connaître au spectateur, ou par une narration, ou par quelque autre adresse de l'art.*"

body. Nor does this anything contradict the opinion of Horace, where he tells us,

> the mind is stirred less by what enters through the ears than by what is brought before the trusty eyes.

For he says immediately after,

> Yet you will not bring on the stage what should be performed behind the scenes, and you will keep much from our sight which the actor may relate with his ready tongue.

Among which many he recounts some:

> So that Medea is not to butcher her boys before the audience, nor evil Atreus cook human flesh on the stage, nor Procne be turned into a bird, nor Cadmus into a serpent, &c.[58]

That is, those actions which by reason of their cruelty will cause aversion in us or, by reason of their impossibility, unbelief, ought either wholly to be avoided by a poet, or only delivered by narration. To which we may have leave to add such as to avoid tumult (as was before hinted), or to reduce the plot into a more reasonable compass of time, or for defect of beauty in them, are rather to be related than presented to the eye. Examples of all these kinds are frequent, not only among all the Ancient, but in the best received of our English poets. We find Ben Jonson using them in his *Magnetic Lady*, where one comes out from dinner, and relates the quarrels and disorders of it to save the undecent appearance of them on the stage, and to abbreviate the story; and this in express imitation of Terence, who had done the same before him in his *Eunuch*, where Pythias makes the like relation of what had happened within at the soldiers' entertainment. The relations likewise of Sejanus's

---

58. *segnius irritant animos demissa per aurem,*
    *quam quae sunt oculis subjecta fidelibus. . . .*
                     *non tamen*
    *digna geri promes in saenam; multaque tolles*
    *ex oculis, quae mox narret facundia præsens. . . .*
    *nec pueros coram populo Medea trucidet,*
    *aut in avem Procne mutetur, Cadmus in anguem, &c.*
                     *Ars poetica*, ll. 180–187.

death, and the prodigies before it, are remarkable; the one of which was hid from sight, to avoid the horror and tumult of the representation; the other, to shun the introducing of things impossible to be believed. In that excellent play the *King and No King*,[59] Fletcher goes yet farther; for the whole unravelling of the plot is done by narration in the fifth act, after the manner of the Ancients; and it moves great concernment in the audience, though it be only a relation of what was done many years before the play. I could multiply other instances, but these are sufficient to prove that there is no error in choosing a subject which requires this sort of narrations; in the ill managing of them, there may.

"But I find I have been too long in this discourse, since the French have many other excellencies not common to us, as that you never see any of their plays end with a conversion, or simple change of will, which is the ordinary way which our poets use to end theirs. It shows little art in the conclusion of a dramatic poem when they, who have hindered the felicity during the four acts, desist from it in the fifth, without some powerful cause to take them off; and though I deny not but such reasons may be found, yet it is a path that is cautiously to be trod, and the poet is to be sure he convinces the audience that the motive is strong enough. As for example, the conversion of the usurer in *The Scornful Lady* seems to me a little forced; for, being an usurer, which implies a lover of money to the highest degree of covetousness (and such the poet has represented him), the account he gives for the sudden change is, that he has been duped by the wild young fellow, which in reason might render him more wary another time, and make him punish himself with harder fare and coarser clothes to get it up again; but that he should look on it as a judgment, and so repent, we may expect to hear of in a sermon, but I should never endure it in a play.

"I pass by this; neither will I insist on the care they take that no person after his first entrance shall ever appear but the business which brings him upon the stage shall be evident; which, if observed, must needs render all the events in the play more natural; for there

59. One of Beaumont and Fletcher's most popular collaborations, first performed in 1611, published in 1619. *The Scornful Lady*, which Dryden mentions in the following paragraph, was another of their collaborative works, first performed and published in 1616.

you see the probability of every accident, in the cause that produced it; and that which appears chance in the play, will seem so reasonable to you that you will there find it almost necessary; so that in the exits of their actors you have a clear account of their purpose and design in the next entrance (though, if the scene be well wrought, the event will commonly deceive you), for there is nothing so absurd, says Corneille,[60] as for an actor to leave the stage only because he has no more to say.

"I should now speak of the beauty of their rhyme, and the just reason I have to prefer that way of writing in tragedies before ours in blank verse; but because it is partly received by us,[61] and therefore not altogether peculiar to them, I will say no more of it in relation to their plays. For our own, I doubt not but it will exceedingly beautify them, and I can see but one reason why it should not generally obtain, that is, because our poets write so ill in it. This, indeed, may prove a more prevailing argument than all others which are used to destroy it, and therefore I am only troubled when great and judicious poets, and those who are acknowledged such, have writ or spoke against it; as for others, they are to be answered by that one sentence of an ancient author: 'But as we are at first inflamed to surpass those whom we consider the most eminent, so, when we have despaired either of surpassing or equalling them, our zeal cools with our hopes: doubtless what one cannot pursue successfully, one ceases to pursue; . . . and setting aside those things in which we cannot excel, we seek for something in which we can succeed.'"[62]

Lisideius concluded in this manner; and Neander, after a little pause, thus answered him:

"I shall grant Lisideius, without much dispute, a great part of what he has urged against us, for I acknowledge the French contrive their plots more regularly, observe the laws of comedy, and

60. In the *Discours des trois unités*.

61. Dryden himself had already begun writing plays in rhyme. *The Rival Ladies* (1664) was partly in rhyme, and *The Indian Queen* (1665), which he wrote in collaboration with Sir Robert Howard, was entirely in rhymed heroic couplets.

62. "*sed ut primo ad consequendos eos quos priores ducimus, accendimur, ita ubi aut præteriri, aut aequari eos posse desperavimus, studium cum spe senescit: quod scilicet, assequi non potest, sequi desinit; . . . præteritoque eo in quo eminere non possumus, aliquid in quo nitamur, conquirimus*" (Paterculus, *Historia romana*, I. 17).

decorum of the stage (to speak generally), with more exactness than the English. Farther, I deny not but he has taxed us justly in some irregularities of ours which he has mentioned; yet, after all, I am of opinion that neither our faults nor their virtues are considerable enough to place them above us.

"For the lively imitation of nature being in the definition of a play, those which best fulfil that law ought to be esteemed superior to the others. 'Tis true, those beauties of the French poesy are such as will raise perfection higher where it is, but are not sufficient to give it where it is not: they are indeed the beauties of a statue, but not of a man, because not animated with the soul of poesy, which is imitation of humour [63] and passions; and this Lisideius himself, or any other, however biassed to their party, cannot but acknowledge, if he will either compare the humours of our comedies, or the characters of our serious plays, with theirs. He that will look upon theirs which have been written till these last ten years, or thereabouts, will find it an hard matter to pick out two or three passable humours amongst them. Corneille himself, their arch-poet, what has he produced except *The Liar*, and you know how it was cried up in France; but when it came upon the English stage, though well translated, and that part of Dorant acted to so much advantage by Mr. Hart [64] as I am confident it never received in its own country, the most favorable to it would not put it in competition with many of Fletcher's or Ben Jonson's. In the rest of Corneille's comedies you have little humour; he tells you himself his way is first to show two lovers in good intelligence with each other; in the working up of the play to embroil them by some mistake, and in the latter end to clear it up.

"But of late years Molière, the younger Corneille, Quinault, and some others, have been imitating of afar off the quick turns and graces of the English stage. They have mixed their serious

63. A comic character's dominating moral trait or temperament. The term was popularized by Ben Jonson and in the Restoration his followers, notably Thomas Shadwell, appropriated the term to apply to the comic sense in general. See Dryden's "Preface to *An Evening's Love*," below, p. 90.

64. Charles Hart, a leading Restoration actor. Corneille's *Le Menteur* (1642) was published in translation in England as *The Mistaken Beauty: or the Liar* in 1685 but was performed in the early 1660's.

plays with mirth, like our tragi-comedies, since the death of Cardinal Richelieu; which Lisideius and many others not observing, have commended that in them for a virtue which they themselves no longer practice. Most of their new plays are, like some of ours, derived from the Spanish novels. There is scarce one of them without a veil, and a trusty Diego, who drolls much after the rate of the *Adventures*.[65] But their humours, if I may grace them with that name, are so thin sown that never above one of them comes up in any play. I dare take upon me to find more variety of them in some one play of Ben Jonson's than in all theirs together; as he who has seen *The Alchemist, The Silent Woman,* or *Bartholomew Fair,* cannot but acknowledge with me.

"I grant the French have performed what was possible on the ground-work of the Spanish plays; what was pleasant before, they have made regular; but there is not above one good play to be writ upon all those plots; they are too much alike to please often, which we need not the experience of our own stage to justify. As for their new way of mingling mirth with serious plot, I do not with Lisideius condemn the thing, though I cannot approve their manner of doing it. He tells us we cannot so speedily recollect ourselves after a scene of great passion and concernment as to pass to another of mirth and humour, and to enjoy it with any relish: but why should he imagine the soul of man more heavy than his senses? Does not the eye pass from an unpleasant object to a pleasant in a much shorter time than is required to this? and does not the unpleasantness of the first commend the beauty of the latter? The old rule of logic might have convinced him that contraries, when placed near, set off each other. A continued gravity keeps the spirit too much bent; we must refresh it sometimes, as we bait upon a journey, that we may go on with greater ease. A scene of mirth mixed with tragedy has the same effect upon us which our music has betwixt the acts; and that we find a relief to us from the best plots and language of the stage, if the discourses have been long. I must therefore have stronger arguments ere I am convinced that compassion and

---

65. *Adventures of Five Hours* (1663), an early Restoration stage hit by Sir Samuel Tuke, was an adaptation of a Spanish play. Diego was a witty servant in the *Adventures.*

mirth in the same subject destroy each other; and in the meantime cannot but conclude, to the honor of our nation, that we have invented, increased, and perfected a more pleasant way of writing for the stage than was ever known to the ancients or moderns of any nation, which is tragi-comedy.

"And this leads me to wonder why Lisideius and many others should cry up the barrenness of the French plots above the variety and copiousness of the English. Their plots are single, they carry on one design which is pushed forward by all the actors, every scene in the play contributing and moving towards it: our plays, besides the main design, have under-plots or by-concernments of less considerable persons and intrigues, which are carried on with the motion of the main plot; just as they say the orb of the fixed stars, and those of the planets, though they have motions of their own, are whirled about by the motion of the *primum mobile* [First Mover] [66] in which they are contained. That similitude expresses much of the English stage; for if contrary motions may be found in nature to agree, if a planet can go east and west at the same time, one way by virtue of his own motion, the other by the force of the First Mover, it will not be difficult to imagine how the under-plot, which is only different, not contrary to the great design, may naturally be conducted along with it.

"Eugenius [67] has already shown us, from the confession of the French poets, that the unity of action is sufficiently preserved if all the imperfect actions of the play are conducing to the main design; but when those petty intrigues of a play are so ill ordered that they have no coherence with the other, I must grant Lisideius has reason to tax that want of due connection; for co-ordination in a play is as dangerous and unnatural as in a State. In the meantime he must acknowledge our variety, if well ordered, will afford a greater pleasure to the audience.

"As for his other argument, that by pursuing one single theme they gain an advantage to express and work up the passions, I

66. The ninth sphere of the Ptolemaic astronomical system, the sphere which gives motion to the rest.
67. An error for "Crites."

wish any example he could bring from them would make it good: for I confess their verses are to me the coldest I have ever read. Neither, indeed, is it possible for them, in the way they take, so to express passion as that the effects of it should appear in the concernment of an audience: their speeches being so many declamations, which tire us with the length; so that instead of persuading us to grieve for their imaginary heroes, we are concerned for our own trouble, as we are in the tedious visits of bad company; we are in pain till they are gone. When the French stage came to be reformed by Cardinal Richelieu, those long harangues were introduced to comply with the gravity of a churchman. Look upon the *Cinna* and the *Pompey*; they are not so properly to be called plays as long discourses of reason of State; and *Polyeucte*[68] in matters of religion is as solemn as the long stops upon our organs. Since that time it is grown into a custom, and their actors speak by the hour-glass, as our parsons do; nay, they account it the grace of their parts, and think themselves disparaged by the poet, if they may not twice or thrice in a play entertain the audience with a speech of an hundred or two hundred lines. I deny not but this may suit well enough with the French; for as we, who are a more sullen people, come to be diverted at our plays; they, who are of an airy and gay temper, come thither to make themselves more serious: and this I conceive to be one reason why comedy is more pleasing to us, and tragedies to them. But to speak generally, it cannot be denied that short speeches and replies are more apt to move the passions and beget concernment in us than the other: for it is unnatural for any one in a gust of passion to speak long together, or for another in the same condition to suffer him without interruption. Grief and passion are like floods raised in little brooks by a sudden rain; they are quickly up; and if the concernment be poured unexpected in upon us, it overflows us: but a long, sober shower gives them leisure to run out as they came in, without troubling the ordinary current. As for comedy, repartee is one of its chiefest graces; the greatest pleasure of the audience is a chase of wit kept up on both sides, and

68. *Cinna, Pompey,* and *Polyeucte* were three of Corneille's earliest, and most famous plays.

swiftly managed. And this our forefathers, if not we, have had in Fletcher's plays, to a much higher degree of perfection than the French poets can arrive at.

"There is another part of Lisideius his discourse, in which he has rather excused our neighbors than commended them; that is, for aiming only to make one person considerable in their plays. 'Tis very true what he has urged, that one character in all plays, even without the poet's care, will have advantage of all the others; and that the design of the whole drama will chiefly depend on it. But this hinders not that there may be more shining characters in the play: many persons of a second magnitude, nay, some so very near, so almost equal to the first, that greatness may be opposed to greatness, and all the persons be made considerable, not only by their quality but their action. 'Tis evident that the more the persons are, the greater will be the variety of the plot. If then the parts are managed so regularly that the beauty of the whole be kept entire, and that the variety become not a perplexed and confused mass of accidents, you will find it infinitely pleasing to be led in a labyrinth of design, where you see some of your way before you, yet discern not the end till you arrive at it. And that all this is practicable, I can produce for examples many of our English plays: as *The Maid's Tragedy*, *The Alchemist*, *The Silent Woman*.[69] I was going to have named *The Fox*, but that the unity of design seems not exactly observed in it, for there appear two actions in the play; the first naturally ending with the fourth act; the second forced from it in the fifth: which yet is the less to be condemned in him, because the disguise of Volpone, though it suited not with his character as a crafty or covetous person, agreed well enough with that of a voluptuary; and by it the poet gained the end he aimed at, the punishment of vice, and the reward of virtue, which that disguise produced. So that to judge equally of it, it was an excellent fifth act, but not so naturally proceeding from the former.

"But to leave this, and pass to the latter part of Lisideius his discourse, which concerns relations, I must acknowledge with him that the French have reason when they hide that part of the action

69. *The Maid's Tragedy* is by Beaumont and Fletcher; the other plays Dryden mentions here are by Ben Jonson.

which would occasion too much tumult upon the stage, and choose rather to have it made known by narration to the audience. Farther, I think it very convenient, for the reasons he has given, that all incredible actions were removed; but whether custom has so insinuated itself into our countrymen, or nature has so formed them to fierceness, I know not; but they will scarcely suffer combats and other objects of horror to be taken from them. And indeed, the indecency of tumults is all which can be objected against fighting: for why may not our imagination as well suffer itself to be deluded with the probability of it, as with any other thing in the play? For my part, I can with as great ease persuade myself that the blows which are struck are given in good earnest, as I can that they who strike them are kings or princes, or those persons which they represent. For objects of incredibility, I would be satisfied from Lisideius whether we have any so removed from all appearance of truth as are those of Corneille's *Andromède*, a play which has been frequented the most of any he has writ? If the Perseus, or the son of a heathen god, the Pegasus, and the Monster, were not capable to choke a strong belief, let him blame any representation of ours hereafter. Those indeed were objects of delight; yet the reason is the same as to the probability: for he makes it not a ballet or masque, but a play, which is to resemble truth. But for death, that it ought not to be represented, I have, besides the arguments alleged by Lisideius, the authority of Ben Jonson, who has forborne it in his tragedies; for both the death of Sejanus and Catiline are related; though in the latter I cannot but observe one irregularity of that great poet: he has removed the scene in the same act from Rome to Catiline's army, and from thence again to Rome; and besides, has allowed a very inconsiderable time, after Catiline's speech, for the striking of the battle, and the return of Petreius, who is to relate the event of it to the Senate: which I should not animadvert on him, who was otherwise a painful observer of τὸ πρέπον, or the decorum of the stage, if he had not used extreme severity in his judgment on the incomparable Shakespeare for the same fault.[70] To conclude

---

70. See Jonson's 1616 Prologue to *Every Man in his Humour*. In the prologue and elsewhere Jonson had criticized many of the same English stage conventions which Lisideius attacks, and with the same reasoning.

on this subject of relations, if we are to be blamed for showing too much of the action, the French are as faulty for discovering too little of it: a mean betwixt both should be observed by every judicious writer, so as the audience may neither be left unsatisfied by not seeing what is beautiful, or shocked by beholding what is either incredible or undecent.

"I hope I have already proved in this discourse that, though we are not altogether so punctual as the French in observing the laws of comedy, yet our errors are so few, and little, and those things wherein we excel them so considerable, that we ought of right to be preferred before them. But what will Lisideius say, if they themselves acknowledge they are too strictly tied up by those laws for breaking which he has blamed the English? I will allege Corneille's words, as I find them in the end of his 'Discourse of the Three Unities': *Il est facile aux spéculatifs d'estre sévères, &c.* ' 'Tis easy for speculative persons to judge severely; but if they would produce to public view ten or twelve pieces of this nature, they would perhaps give more latitude to the rules than I have done, when by experience they had known how much we are bound up and constrained by them, and how many beauties of the stage they banished from it.' To illustrate a little what he has said, by their servile observations of the unities of time and place, and integrity of scenes, they have brought on themselves that dearth of plot, and narrowness of imagination, which may be observed in all their plays. How many beautiful accidents might naturally happen in two or three days, which cannot arrive with any probability in the compass of twenty-four hours? There is time to be allowed also for maturity of design which, amongst great and prudent persons such as are often represented in tragedy, cannot, with any likelihood of truth, be brought to pass at so short a warning. Farther, by tying themselves strictly to the unity of place and unbroken scenes, they are forced many times to omit some beauties which cannot be shown where the act began; but might, if the scene were interrupted, and the stage cleared for the persons to enter in another place; and therefore the French poets are often forced upon absurdities: for if the act begins in a chamber, all the persons in the play must have some business or other to come thither, or else they are not to be

shown that act, and sometimes their characters are very unfitting
to appear there. As, suppose it were the King's bed-chamber, yet
the meanest man in the tragedy must come and dispatch his
business there, rather than in the lobby or courtyard (which is
fitter for him), for fear the stage should be cleared and the scenes
broken. Many times they fall by it into a greater inconvenience;
for they keep their scenes unbroken, and yet change the place;
as in one of their newest plays, where the act begins in the street.[71]
There a gentleman is to meet his friend; he sees him with his man,
coming out from his father's house; they talk together, and the
first goes out: the second, who is a lover, has made an appointment
with his mistress; she appears at the window, and then we are to
imagine the scene lies under it. This gentleman is called away,
and leaves his servant with his mistress; presently her father is
heard from within; the young lady is afraid the servingman should
be discovered, and thrusts him in through a door which is supposed
to be her closet. After this, the father enters to the daughter, and
now the scene is in a house; for he is seeking from one room to
another for this poor Philipin, or French Diego, who is heard
from within, drolling and breaking many a miserable conceit upon
his sad condition. In this ridiculous manner the play goes on, the
stage being never empty all the while: so that the street, the window,
the two houses, and the closet, are made to walk about, and the
persons to stand still. Now what, I beseech you, is more easy than to
write a regular French play, or more difficult than to write an
irregular English one, like those of Fletcher or of Shakespeare?

"If they content themselves, as Corneille did, with some flat
design which, like an ill riddle, is found out ere it be half proposed;
such plots we can make every way regular, as easily as they; but
whene'er they endeavor to rise to any quick turns and counterturns
of plot, as some of them have attempted since Corneille's plays have
been less in vogue, you see they write as irregularly as we, though
they cover it more speciously. Hence the reason is perspicuous why
no French plays, when translated, have, or ever can succeed upon
the English stage. For if you consider the plots, our own are fuller
of variety; if the writing, ours are more quick and fuller of spirit;

71. Thomas Corneille, *l'Amour à la mode* (1651).

and therefore 'tis a strange mistake in those who decry the way of writing plays in verse, as if the English therein imitated the French. We have borrowed nothing from them; our plots are weaved in English looms: we endeavor therein to follow the variety and greatness of characters which are derived to us from Shakespeare and Fletcher; the copiousness and well-knitting of the intrigues we have from Jonson; and for the verse itself we have English precedents of elder date than any of Corneille's plays: (not to name our old comedies before Shakespeare, which were all writ in verse of six feet, or alexandrines, such as the French now use). I can show in Shakespeare many scenes of rhyme together, and the like in Ben Jonson's tragedies: in *Catiline* and *Sejanus* sometimes thirty or forty lines, I mean besides the Chorus, or the monologues, which, by the way, showed Ben no enemy to this way of writing, especially if you look upon his *Sad Shepherd*, which goes sometimes upon rhyme, sometimes upon blank verse, like an horse who eases himself upon trot and amble. You find him likewise commending Fletcher's pastoral of *The Faithful Shepherdess*, which is for the most part rhyme, though not refined to that purity to which it hath since been brought. And these examples are enough to clear us from a servile imitation of the French.

"But to return from whence I have digressed, I dare boldly affirm these two things of the English drama: first, that we have many plays of ours as regular as any of theirs, and which, besides, have more variety of plot and characters; and secondly, that in most of the irregular plays of Shakespeare or Fletcher (for Ben Jonson's are for the most part regular) there is a more masculine fancy and greater spirit in all the writing than there is in any of the French. I could produce, even in Shakespeare's and Fletcher's works, some plays which are almost exactly formed; as *The Merry Wives of Windsor*, and *The Scornful Lady*; but because (generally speaking) Shakespeare, who writ first, did not perfectly observe the laws of comedy, and Fletcher, who came nearer to perfection, yet through carelessness made many faults, I will take the pattern of a perfect play from Ben Jonson, who was a careful and learned observer of the dramatic laws, and from all his comedies I shall select *The Silent Woman*; of which I will make a short examen, according to those rules which the French observe."

As Neander was beginning to examine *The Silent Woman*, Eugenius, looking earnestly upon him: "I beseech you, Neander," said he, "gratify the company and me in particular so far, as before you speak of the play, to give us a character of the author; and tell us frankly your opinion, whether you do not think all writers, both French and English, ought to give place to him."

"I fear," replied Neander, "that in obeying your commands I shall draw a little envy upon myself. Besides, in performing them, it will be first necessary to speak somewhat of Shakespeare and Fletcher, his rivals in poesy; and one of them, in my opinion, at least his equal, perhaps his superior.

"To begin, then, with Shakespeare: he was the man who of all modern, and perhaps ancient poets, had the largest and most comprehensive soul. All the images of nature were still present to him, and he drew them not laboriously, but luckily; when he describes anything, you more than see it, you feel it too. Those who accuse him to have wanted learning give him the greater commendation: he was naturally learned; he needed not the spectacles of books to read nature; he looked inwards, and found her there. I cannot say he is everywhere alike; were he so, I should do him injury to compare him with the greatest of mankind. He is many times flat, insipid; his comic wit degenerating into clenches, his serious swelling into bombast. But he is always great when some great occasion is presented to him; no man can say he ever had a fit subject for his wit, and did not then raise himself as high above the rest of poets,

as cypresses often do among bending osiers.[72]

The consideration of this made Mr. Hales of Eton say that there was no subject of which any poet ever writ, but he would produce it much better treated of in Shakespeare; and however others are now generally preferred before him, yet the age wherein he lived, which had contemporaries with him Fletcher and Jonson, never equalled them to him in their esteem. And in the last King's court, when Ben's reputation was at highest, Sir John Suckling, and with him the greater part of the courtiers, set our Shakespeare far above him.

72. "*quantum lenta solent inter viburna cupressi*" (Virgil, *Eclogues*, I. 25).

"Beaumount and Fletcher, of whom I am next to speak, had, with the advantage of Shakespeare's wit, which was their precedent, great natural gifts improved by study; Beaumont especially being so accurate a judge of plays that Ben Jonson, while he lived, submitted all his writing to his censure, and, 'tis thought, used his judgment in correcting, if not contriving, all his plots. What value he had for him, appears by the verses he writ to him; and therefore I need speak no farther of it. The first play which brought Fletcher and him in esteem was their *Philaster*: for before that, they had written two or three very unsuccessfully, as the like is reported of Ben Jonson before he writ *Every Man in his Humour*. Their plots were generally more regular than Shakespeare's, especially those which were made before Beaumont's death; and they understood and imitated the conversation of gentlemen much better; whose wild debaucheries, and quickness of wit in repartees, no poet can ever paint as they have done. This humour of which Ben Jonson derived from particular persons, they made it not their business to describe: they represented all the passions very lively, but above all, love. I am apt to believe the English language in them arrived to its highest perfection: what words have since been taken in, are rather superfluous than necessary. Their plays are now the most pleasant and frequent entertainments of the stage; two of theirs being acted through the year for one of Shakespeare's or Jonson's: the reason is because there is a certain gaiety in their comedies, and pathos in their more serious plays, which suits generally with all men's humours. Shakespeare's language is likewise a little obsolete, and Ben Jonson's wit comes short of theirs.

"As for Jonson, to whose character I am now arrived, if we look upon him while he was himself (for his last plays were but his dotages), I think him the most learned and judicious writer which any theater ever had. He was a most severe judge of himself as well as others. One cannot say he wanted wit, but rather that he was frugal of it. In his works you find little to retrench or alter. Wit, and language, and humour also in some measure, we had before him; but something of art was wanting to the drama till he came. He managed his strength to more advantage than any who preceded him. You seldom find him making love in any of his scenes, or endeavoring to move the passions; his genius was too sullen and saturnine to do it gracefully, especially when he knew he came after those who had performed both to such an height. Humour was his proper sphere; and in that he delighted most to represent mechanic people. He was deeply conversant in the Ancients, both Greek and Latin, and he borrowed boldly from them: there is scarce a poet or historian among the Roman authors of those times whom he has not translated in *Sejanus* and *Catiline*. But he has done his robberies so openly that one may see he fears not to be taxed by any law. He invades authors like a monarch, and what would be theft in other poets is only victory in him. With the spoils of these writers he so represents old Rome to us, in its rites, ceremonies, and customs, that if one of their poets had written either of his tragedies, we had seen less of it than in him. If there was any fault in his language, 'twas that he weaved it too closely and laboriously in his serious plays: perhaps, too, he did a little too much romanize our tongue, leaving the words which he translated almost as much Latin as he found them: wherein, though he learnedly followed the idiom of their language, he did not enough comply with ours. If I would compare him with Shakespeare, I must acknowledge him the more correct poet, but Shakespeare the greater wit. Shakespeare was the Homer, or father of our dramatic poets; Jonson was the Virgil, the pattern of elaborate writing; I admire him, but I love Shakespeare. To conclude of him, as he has given us the most correct plays, so in the precepts which he has laid down in his *Discoveries*, we have as many and profitable rules for perfecting the stage as any wherewith the French can furnish us.

"Having thus spoken of the author, I proceed to the examination of his comedy, *The Silent Woman*.

### Examen of the Silent Woman.

"To begin first with the length of the action, it is so far from exceeding the compass of a natural day that it takes not up an artificial one. 'Tis all included in the limits of three hours and an half, which is no more than is required for the presentment on the stage. A beauty perhaps not much observed; if it had, we should not have looked on the Spanish translation of *Five Hours* [73] with so

73. See note 65 above.

much wonder. The scene of it is laid in London; the latitude of place is almost as little as you can imagine: for it lies all within the compass of two houses, and after the first act, in one. The continuity of scenes is observed more than in any of our plays, excepting his own *Fox* and *Alchemist*. They are not broken above twice or thrice at most in the whole comedy; and in the two best of Corneille's plays, the *Cid* and *Cinna*, they are interrupted once apiece. The action of the play is entirely one; the end or aim of which is the settling Morose's estate on Dauphine. The intrigue of it is the greatest and most noble of any pure unmixed comedy in any language; you see in it many persons of various characters and humours, and all delightful: as first, Morose, or an old man, to whom all noise but his own talking is offensive. Some who would be thought critics say this humour of his is forced: but to remove that objection, we may consider him first to be naturally of a delicate hearing, as many are to whom all sharp sounds are unpleasant; and secondly, we may attribute much of it to the peevishness of his age, or the wayward authority of an old man in his own house, where he may make himself obeyed; and this the poet seems to allude to in his name *Morose*. Besides this, I am assured from divers persons that Ben Jonson was actually acquainted with such a man, one altogether as ridiculous as he is here represented. Others say it is not enough to find one man of such an humour; it must be common to more, and the more common the more natural. To prove this, they instance in the best of comical characters, Falstaff: there are many men resembling him; old, fat, merry, cowardly, drunken, amorous, vain, and lying. But to convince these people, I need but tell them that humour is the ridiculous extravagance of conversation, wherein one man differs from all others. If then it be common, or communicated to many, how differs it from other men's? or what indeed causes it to be ridiculous so much as the singularity of it? As for Falstaff, he is not properly one humour, but a miscellany of humours or images, drawn from so many several men: that wherein he is singular in his wit, or those things he says *praeter expectatum*, unexpected by the audience; his quick evasions when you imagine him surprised, which, as they are extreme-ly diverting of themselves, so receive a great addition from his

person; for the very sight of such an unwieldy, old, debauched
fellow is a comedy alone. And here, having a place so proper for
it, I cannot but enlarge somewhat upon this subject of humour
into which I am fallen. The Ancients had little of it in their comedies; for the τὸ γελοῖον [ridiculous] of the Old Comedy, of which
Aristophanes was chief, was not so much to imitate a man as to
make the people laugh at some odd conceit which had commonly
somewhat of unnatural or obscene in it. Thus, when you see
Socrates brought upon the stage, you are not to imagine him made
ridiculous by the imitation of his actions, but rather by making
him perform something very unlike himself: something so childish
and absurd as, by comparing it with the gravity of the true Socrates,
makes a ridiculous object for the spectators. In their New Comedy,
which succeeded, the poets sought indeed to express the *ethos*
[character], as in their tragedies the *pathos* [emotions] of mankind.
But this *ethos* contained only the general characters of men and
manners; as old men, lovers, serving-men, courtesans, parasites,
and such other persons as we see in their comedies; all which they
made alike: that is, one old man or father, one lover, one courtesan,
so like another as if the first of them had begot the rest of every sort:
'each one exactly like the other'.[74] The same custom they observed
likewise in their tragedies. As for the French, though they have the
word *humeur* among them, yet they have small use of it in their
comedies or farces; they being but ill imitations of the *ridiculum*,
or that which stirred up laughter in the Old Comedy. But among
the English 'tis otherwise: where by humour is meant some extravagant habit, passion, or affection, particular (as I said before) to
some one person, by the oddness of which he is immediately
distinguished from the rest of men; which being lively and naturally
represented, most frequently begets that malicious pleasure in the
audience which is testified by laughter; as all things which are
deviations from common customs are ever the aptest to produce it:
though, by the way, this laughter is only accidental, as the person
represented is fantastic or bizarre; but pleasure is essential to it,
as the imitation of what is natural. The description of these humours,
drawn from the knowledge and observation of particular persons,

74. "*ex homine hunc natum dicas*" (Terence, *Eunuch*, 1. 460).

was the peculiar genius and talent of Ben Jonson; to whose play I now return.

"Besides Morose, there are at least nine or ten different characters and humours in *The Silent Woman*, all which persons have several concernments of their own, yet are all used by the poet to the conducting of the main design to perfection. I shall not waste time in commending the writing of this play, but I will give you my opinion that there is more wit and acuteness of fancy in it than in any of Ben Jonson's. Besides, that he has here described the conversation of gentlemen in the persons of True-Wit and his friends, with more gaiety, air, and freedom, than in the rest of his comedies. For the contrivance of the plot, 'tis extreme elaborate, and yet withal easy; for the λύσις, or untying of it, 'tis so admirable that, when it is done, no one of the audience would think the poet could have missed it; and yet it was concealed so much before the last scene that any other way would sooner have entered into your thoughts. But I dare not take upon me to commend the fabric of it, because it is altogether so full of art that I must unravel every scene in it to commend it as I ought. And this excellent contrivance is still the more to be admired because 'tis comedy, where the persons are only of common rank, and their business private, not elevated by passions or high concernments as in serious plays. Here every one is a proper judge of all he sees; nothing is represented but that with which he daily converses: so that by consequence all faults lie open to discovery, and few are pardonable. 'Tis this which Horace has judiciously observed:

> It is thought that comedy, which draws its themes from daily life, calls for little labor; but it calls for more, as the indulgence allowed is less.[75]

But our poet, who was not ignorant of these difficulties, had prevailed himself of all advantages; as he who designs a large leap takes his rise from the highest ground. One of these advantages is that which Corneille has laid down as the greatest which can arrive to any poem, and which he himself could never compass

75. *creditur, ex medio quia res arcessit, habere*
    *sudoris minimum; sed habet Comedia tanto*
    *plus oneris, quanto veniae minus.*
    *Epistles,* II. i. 168–170.

above thrice in all his plays; *viz.* the making choice of some signal
and long-expected day, whereon the action of the play is to
depend. This day was that designed by Dauphine for the settling
of his uncle's estate upon him; which to compass, he contrives to
marry him. That the marriage had been plotted by him long beforehand is made evident by what he tells True-Wit in the second act,
that in one moment he had destroyed what he had been raising
many months.

"There is another artifice of the poet which I cannot here omit,
because by the frequent practice of it in his comedies he has left
it to us almost as a rule: that is, when he has any character or humour
wherein he would show a *coup de maistre*, or his highest skill, he
recommends it to your observation by a pleasant description of it
before the person first appears. Thus, in *Bartholomew Fair* he gives
you the pictures of Numps and Cokes, and in this those of Daw,
Lafoole, Morose, and the Collegiate Ladies; all which you hear
described before you see them. So that before they come upon
the stage you have a longing expectation of them, which prepares
you to receive them favorably; and when they are there, even from
their first appearance you are so far acquainted with them that
nothing of their humour is lost to you.

"I will observe yet one thing further of this admirable plot:
the business of it rises in every act. The second is greater than the
first, the third than the second, and so forward to the fifth. There
too you see, till the very last scene, new difficulties arising to ob-
struct the action of the play; and when the audience is brought into
despair that the business can naturally be effected, then, and not
before, the discovery is made. But that the poet might entertain
you with more variety all this while, he reserves some new characters
to show you, which he opens not till the second and third act.
In the second, Morose, Daw, the Barber, and Otter; in the third,
the Collegiate Ladies: all which he moves afterwards in by-walks,
or under-plots, as diversions to the main design, lest it should grow
tedious, though they are still naturally joined with it, and somewhere
or other subservient to it. Thus, like a skilful chess-player, by little
and little he draws out his men, and makes his pawns of use to his
greater persons.

"If this comedy, and some others of his, were translated into French prose (which would now be no wonder to them, since Molière has lately given them plays out of verse which have not displeased them), I believe the controversy would soon be decided betwixt the two nations, even making them the judges. But we need not call our heroes to our aid; be it spoken to the honor of the English, our nation can never want in any age such who are able to dispute the empire of wit with any people in the universe. And though the fury of a civil war, and power for twenty years together abandoned to a barbarous race of men, enemies of all good learning, had buried the Muses under the ruins of monarchy; yet, with the restoration of our happiness, we see revived poesy lifting up its head, and already shaking off the rubbish which lay so heavy on it. We have seen since his Majesty's return many dramatic poems which yield not to those of any foreign nation, and which deserve all laurels but the English. I will set aside flattery and envy: it cannot be denied but we have had some little blemish either in the plot or writing of all those plays which have been made within these seven years (and perhaps there is no nation in the world so quick to discern them, or so difficult to pardon them, as ours): yet if we can persuade ourselves to use the candor of that poet who (though the most severe of critics) has left us this caution by which to moderate our censures:

> when there are numerous beauties in a poem, I will not be offended by a few blemishes; [76]

if, in consideration of their many and great beauties, we can wink at some slight and little imperfections; if we, I say, can be thus equal to ourselves, I ask no favor from the French. And if I do not venture upon any particular judgment of our late plays, 'tis out of the consideration which an ancient writer gives me: *vivorum, ut magna admiratio, ita censura difficilis*:[77] betwixt the extremes of ad-

76. *ubi plura nitent in carmine, non ego paucis*
    *offendar maculis.*
          Horace, *Ars poetica*, ll. 351–352.
77. Paterculus, *Historia romana*, II. 36.

miration and malice, 'tis hard to judge uprightly of the living.
Only I think it may be permitted me to say that as it is no lessening
to us to yield to some plays, and those not many, of our own nation
in the last age, so can it be no addition to pronounce of our present
poets that they have far surpassed all the Ancients, and the modern
writers of other countries."

This, my Lord, was the substance of what was then spoke on that
occasion; and Lisideius, I think, was going to reply, when he was
prevented thus by Crites: "I am confident," said he, "the most
material things that can be said have been already urged on either
side; if they have not, I must beg of Lisideius that he will defer
his answer till another time: for I confess I have a joint quarrel to
you both, because you have concluded, without any reason given
for it, that rhyme is proper for the stage. I will not dispute how
ancient it hath been among us to write this way; perhaps our
ancestors knew no better till Shakespeare's time. I will grant it was
not altogether left by him, and that Fletcher and Ben Jonson used it
frequently in their pastorals, and sometimes in other plays. Farther,
I will not argue whether we received it originally from our own
countrymen, or from the French; for that is an inquiry of as little
benefit as theirs who, in the midst of the great plague, were not so
solicitous to provide against it as to know whether we had it from
the malignity of our own air, or by transportation from Holland.
I have therefore only to affirm that it is not allowable in serious
plays; for comedies, I find you already concluding with me. To
prove this, I might satisfy myself to tell you how much in vain it
is for you to strive against the stream of the people's inclination,
the greatest part of which are prepossessed so much with those
excellent plays of Shakespeare, Fletcher, and Ben Jonson (which
have been written out of rhyme) that except you could bring them
such as were written better in it, and those too by persons of equal
reputation with them, it will be impossible for you to gain your
cause with them who will still be judges. This it is to which, in fine,
all your reasons must submit. The unanimous consent of an audience is so powerful that even Julius Caesar (as Macrobius reports
of him), when he was perpetual dictator, was not able to balance it

on the other side. But when Laberius, a Roman knight, at his request contended in the mime with another poet, he was forced to cry out, 'you have been beaten, Laberius, for all my favor.'[78]

"But I will not on this occasion take the advantage of the greater number, but only urge such reasons against rhyme as I find in the writings of those who have argued for the other way. First, then, I am of opinion that rhyme is unnatural in a play, because dialogue there is presented as the effect of sudden thought. For a play is the imitation of nature; and since no man without premeditation speaks in rhyme, neither ought he to do it on the stage. This hinders not but the fancy may be there elevated to an higher pitch of thought than it is in ordinary discourse; for there is a probability that men of excellent and quick parts may speak noble things *ex tempore*: but those thoughts are never fettered with the numbers or sound of verse without study, and therefore it cannot be but unnatural to present the most free way of speaking in that which is the most constrained. For this reason, says Aristotle, 'tis best to write tragedy in that kind of verse which is the least such, or which is nearest prose: and this amongst the Ancients was the iambic, and with us is blank verse, or the measure of verse kept exactly without rhyme. These numbers therefore are fittest for a play; the others for a paper of verses or a poem; blank verse being as much below them as rhyme is improper for the drama. And if it be objected that neither are blank verses made *ex tempore*, yet, as nearest nature, they are still to be preferred.

"But there are two particular exceptions which many besides myself have had to verse; by which it will appear yet more plainly how improper it is in plays. And the first of them is grounded on that very reason for which some have commended rhyme: they say the quickness of repartees in argumentative scenes receives an ornament from verse. Now what is more unreasonable than to imagine that a man should not only light upon the wit, but the rhyme too upon the sudden? This nicking of him who spoke before, both in sound and measure, is so great an happiness that you must at least suppose the persons of your play to be born poets, 'all

78. *"etiam favente me victus es, Laberi"* (Macrobius, *Saturnalia*, II. 7).

Arcadians, ready both to sing and to respond,'[79] they must have arrived to the degree of *quicquid conabar dicere*: to make verses almost whether they will or no. If they are any thing below this, it will look rather like the design of two than the answer of one: it will appear that your actors hold intelligence together, that they perform their tricks like fortune-tellers, by confederacy. The hand of art will be too visible in it against that maxim of all professions, *ars est celare artem*, that it is the greatest perfection of art to keep itself undiscovered. Nor will it serve you to object that, however you manage it, 'tis still known to be a play; and, consequently, the dialogue of two persons understood to be the labor of one poet. For a play is still an imitation of nature; we know we are to be deceived, and we desire to be so; but no man ever was deceived but with a probability of truth, for who will suffer a gross lie to be fastened on him? Thus we sufficiently understand that the scenes which represent cities and countries to us are not really such, but only painted on boards and canvas: but shall that excuse the ill painture or designment of them? Nay, rather ought they not to be labored with so much the more diligence and exactness, to help the imagination? since the mind of man does naturally tend to, and seek after truth; and therefore the nearer any thing comes to the imitation of it, the more it pleases.

"Thus, you see, your rhyme is uncapable of expressing the greatest thoughts naturally, and the lowest it cannot with any grace: for what is more unbenefitting the majesty of verse than to call a servant, or bid a door be shut, in rhyme? And yet this miserable necessity you are forced upon. But verse, you say, circumscribes a quick and luxuriant fancy, which would extend itself too far on every subject, did not the labor which is required to well turned and polished rhyme set bounds to it. Yet this argument, if granted, would only prove that we may write better in verse, but not more naturally. Neither is it able to evince that: for he who wants judgment to confine his fancy in blank verse, may want it as much in rhyme; and he who has it will avoid errors in both kinds. Latin verse was as great a confinement to the imagination of those poets as rhyme to ours; and yet you find Ovid saying too much on every subject.

79. "*arcades omnes, et cantare pares, et respondere parati*" (Virgil, *Eclogues*, vii, 4–5).

'He does not know' (says Seneca) 'when to leave well enough alone':[80] of which he gives you one famous instance in his description of the deluge:

> *Omnia pontus erat, deerant quoque litora ponto.*
> Now all was sea, nor had that sea a shore.

Thus Ovid's fancy was not limited by verse, and Virgil needed not verse to have bounded his.

"In our own language we see Ben Jonson confining himself to what ought to be said, even in the liberty of blank verse; and yet Corneille, the most judicious of the French poets, is still varying the same sense an hundred ways, and dwelling eternally on the same subject, though confined by rhyme. Some other exceptions I have to verse; but being these I have named are for the most part already public, I conceive it reasonable they should first be answered."

"It concerns me less than any," said Neander (seeing he had ended), "to reply to this discourse; because when I should have proved that verse may be natural in plays, yet I should always be ready to confess that those which I have written in this kind come short of that perfection which is required. Yet since you are pleased I should undertake this province, I will do it, though with all imaginable respect and deference both to that person from whom you have borrowed your strongest arguments, and to whose judgment, when I have said all, I finally submit. But before I proceed to answer your objections, I must first remember you that I exclude all comedy from my defense; and next that I deny not but blank verse may be also used, and content myself only to assert that in serious plays, where the subject and characters are great, and the plot unmixed with mirth, which might allay or divert these concernments which are produced, rhyme is there as natural, and more effectual than blank verse.

"And now having laid down this as a foundation, to begin with Crites, I must crave leave to tell him that some of his arguments against rhyme reach no farther than, from the faults or defects of

---

80. "*Nescivit quod bene cessit relinquere*" (Marcus Seneca, *Controversiae*, ix. 5). The example Dryden cites is from another Seneca, Lucius Seneca, the philosopher.

ill rhyme, to conclude against the use of it in general. May not I conclude against blank verse by the same reason? If the words of some poets who write in it are either ill chosen, or ill placed (which makes not only rhyme, but all kind of verse in any language un-natural) shall I, for their vicious affectation, condemn those excellent lines of Fletcher which are written in that kind? Is there anything in rhyme more constrained than this line in blank verse:

I heaven invoke, and strong resistance make?

where you see both the clauses are placed unnaturally, that is, contrary to the common way of speaking, and that without the excuse of a rhyme to cause it: yet you would think me very ridiculous if I should accuse the stubbornness of blank verse for this, and not rather the stiffness of the poet. Therefore, Crites, you must either prove that words, though well chosen and duly placed, yet render not rhyme natural in itself; or that however natural and easy the rhyme may be, yet it is not proper for a play. If you insist on the former part, I would ask you what other conditions are required to make rhyme natural in itself, besides an election of apt words, and a right disposing of them? For the due choice of your words ex-presses your sense naturally, and the due placing them adapts the rhyme to it. If you object that one verse may be made for the sake of another, though both the words and rhyme be apt, I answer it cannot possibly so fall out; for either there is a dependence of sense betwixt the first line and the second, or there is none: if there be that connection, then in the natural position of the words the latter line must of necessity flow from the former; if there be no dependence, yet still the due ordering of words makes the last line as natural in itself as the other: so that the necessity of a rhyme never forces any but bad or lazy writers to say what they would not otherwise. 'Tis true, there is both care and art required to write in verse. A good poet never concludes upon the first line till he has sought out such a rhyme as may fit the sense, already prepared to heighten the second: many times the close of the sense falls into the middle of the next verse, or farther off, and he may often prevail himself of the same advantages in English which Virgil had in Latin: he may break off in the hemistich, and begin another line. Indeed, the not observing these two last things makes plays which are writ in verse so tedious: for though, most commonly, the sense is to be confined to the couplet, yet nothing that does *perpetuo tenore fluere*, run in the same channel, can please always. 'Tis like the murmuring of a stream which, not varying in the fall, causes at first attention, at last drowsiness. Variety of cadences is the best rule, the greatest help to the actors, and refreshment to the audience.

"If then verse may be made natural in itself, how becomes it improper to a play? You say the stage is the representation of nature, and no man in ordinary conversation speaks in rhyme. But you foresaw when you said this that it might be answered: neither does any man speak in blank verse, or in measure without rhyme. Therefore you concluded, that which is nearest nature is still to be preferred. But you took no notice that rhyme might be made as natural as blank verse by the well placing of the words, &c. All the difference between them, when they are both correct, is the sound in one, which the other wants; and if so, the sweetness of it, and all the advantage resulting from it, which are handled in the preface to *The Rival Ladies*,[81] will yet stand good. As for that place of Aristotle, where he says plays should be writ in that kind of verse which is nearest prose, it makes little for you, blank verse being properly but measured prose. Now measure alone, in any modern language, does not constitute verse; those of the Ancients in Greek and Latin consisted in quantity of words, and a determinate number of feet. But when, by the inundation of the Goths and Vandals into Italy, new languages were brought in, and barbarously mingled with the Latin (of which the Italian, Spanish, French, and ours, made out of them and the Teutonic, are dialects), a new way of poesy was practiced; new, I say, in those countries, for in all probability it was that of the conquerors in their own nations. This new way consisted in measure, or number of feet, and rhyme; the sweetness of rhyme, and observation of accent, supplying the place of quantity in words, which could neither exactly be observed by those barbarians, who knew not the rules of it, neither was it

81. Dryden's first published play (1664), partly in rhyme. Neander repeats many of the arguments justifying rhymed dramatic verse in the preface to the play.

suitable to their tongues, as it had been to the Greek and Latin. No man is tied in modern poesy to observe any farther rule in the feet of his verse, but that they be dissyllables; whether spondee, trochee, or iambic, it matters not; only he is obliged to rhyme. Neither do the Spanish, French, Italian, or Germans acknowledge at all, or very rarely, any such kind of poesy as blank verse amongst them. Therefore, at most 'tis but a poetic prose, a *sermo pedestris*; and as such, most fit for comedies, where I acknowledge rhyme to be improper. Farther, as to that quotation of Aristotle, our couplet verses may be rendered as near prose as blank verse itself, by using those advantages I lately named, as breaks in a hemistich, or running the sense into another line, thereby making art and order appear as loose and free as nature: or not tying ourselves to couplets strictly, we may use the benefit of the Pindaric way practiced in *The Siege of Rhodes*;[82] where the numbers vary, and the rhyme is disposed carelessly, and far from often chiming. Neither is that other advantage of the Ancients to be despised, of changing the kind of verse when they please with the change of the scene, or some new entrance; for they confine not themselves always to iambics, but extend their liberty to all lyric numbers, and sometimes even to hexameter. But I need not go so far to prove that rhyme, as it succeeds to all other offices of Greek and Latin verse, so especially to this of plays, since the custom of all nations at this day confirms it: all the French, Italian, and Spanish tragedies are generally writ in it; and sure the universal consent of the most civilized parts of the world ought in this, as it doth in other customs, include the rest.

"But perhaps you may tell me I have proposed such a way to make rhyme natural, and consequently proper to plays, as is unpracticable, and that I shall scarce find six or eight lines together in any play, where the words are so placed and chosen as is required to make it natural. I answer, no poet need constrain himself at all times to it. It is enough he makes it his general rule; for I deny not but sometimes there may be a greatness in placing the words otherwise; and sometimes they may sound better, sometimes also the

82. A play by Sir William Davenant (1656) which was acknowledged by Dryden and others to be the prototype of Restoration heroic drama.

variety itself is excuse enough. But if, for the most part, the words be placed as they are in the negligence of prose, it is sufficient to denominate the way practicable; for we esteem that to be such, which in the trial oftener succeeds than misses. And thus far you may find the practice made good in many plays: where you do not, remember still that if you cannot find six natural rhymes together, it will be as hard for you to produce as many lines in blank verse, even among the greatest of our poets, against which I cannot make some reasonable exception.

"And this, Sir, calls to my remembrance the beginning of your discourse, where you told us we should never find the audience favorable to this kind of writing till we could produce as good plays in rhyme as Ben Jonson, Fletcher, and Shakespeare had writ out of it. But it is to raise envy to the living, to compare them with the dead. They are honored, and almost adored by us, as they deserve; neither do I know any so presumptuous of themselves as to contend with them. Yet give me leave to say thus much, without injury to their ashes, that not only we shall never equal them, but they could never equal themselves, were they to rise and write again. We acknowledge them our fathers in wit; but they have ruined their estates themselves before they came to their children's hands. There is scarce an humour, a character, or any kind of plot, which they have not blown upon: all comes sullied or wasted to us: and were they to entertain this age, they could not make so plenteous treatments out of such decayed fortunes. This therefore will be a good argument to us either not to write at all, or to attempt some other way. There is no bays to be expected in their walks: 'I must attempt a way, whereby I too may rise from the earth.'[83]

"This way of writing in verse they have only left free to us; our age is arrived to a perfection in it which they never knew; and which, if we may guess by what of theirs we have seen in verse (as *The Faithful Shepherdess*, and *Sad Shepherd*)[84] 'tis probable they never could have reached. For the genius of every age is different; and though ours excel in this, I deny not but that to imitate nature in

---

83. "*tentanda via est, qua me quoque possum tollere humo*" (Virgil, *Georgics*, III. 8–9).

84. The first play is John Fletcher's, the second, which was unfinished, is by Jonson.

that perfection which they did in prose, is a greater commendation than to write in verse exactly. As for what you have added, that the people are not generally inclined to like this way; if it were true, it would be no wonder that betwixt the shaking off an old habit, and the introducing of a new, there should be difficulty. Do we not see them stick to Hopkins' and Sternhold's psalms, and forsake those of David, I mean Sandys his translation of them?[85] If by the people you understand the multitude, the *hoi polloi*, 'tis no matter what they think; they are sometimes in the right, sometimes in the wrong; their judgment is a mere lottery. 'It is where the common people think they are right that they are wrong.'[86] Horace says it of the vulgar, judging poesy. But if you mean the mixed audience of the populace and the noblesse, I dare confidently affirm that a great part of the latter sort are already favorable to verse; and that no serious plays written since the King's return have been more kindly received by them than *The Siege of Rhodes*, the *Mustapha*, *The Indian Queen*, and *Indian Emperor*.[87]

"But I come now to the inference of your first argument. You said the dialogue of plays is presented as the effect of sudden thought, but no man speaks suddenly, or *ex tempore*, in rhyme; and you inferred from thence that rhyme, which you acknowledge to be proper to epic poesy, cannot equally be proper to dramatic, unless we could suppose all men born so much more than poets that verses should be made in them, not by them.

"It has been formerly urged by you, and confessed by me, that since no man spoke any kind of verse *ex tempore*, that which was nearest nature was to be preferred. I answer you, therefore, by distinguishing betwixt what is nearest to the nature of comedy, which is the imitation of common persons and ordinary speaking, and what is nearest the nature of a serious play: this last is indeed the representation of nature, but 'tis nature wrought up to an higher

85. The metrical version of the Psalms by John Hopkins and Thomas Sternhold was far more popular than the superior translation by George Sandys.

86. "*Est ubi rectè putat, est ubi peccat*" (misquoted from *Epistles*, II. i. 63).

87. Sir William Davenant, *The Siege of Rhodes*, *Part I* (1656); Roger Boyle, Earl of Orrery, *Mustapha* (1665); Dryden and Sir Robert Howard, *The Indian Queen* (1664); Dryden, *The Indian Emperor* (1665). The dates given are those of first performance.

pitch. The plot, the characters, the wit, the passions, the descriptions, are all exalted above the level of common converse, as high as the imagination of the poet can carry them with proportion to verisimility. Tragedy, we know, is wont to image to us the minds and fortunes of noble persons; and to portray these exactly, heroic rhyme is nearest nature, as being the noblest kind of modern verse.

> For Thyestes' supper deigns to be narrated in the language of private life, language unworthy of the tragic style,[88]

(says Horace). And in another place,

> Tragedy holds it unworthy to babble trivial verses.[89]

Blank verse is acknowledged to be too low for a poem, nay more, for a paper of verses; but if too low for an ordinary sonnet, how much more for tragedy, which is by Aristotle, in the dispute betwixt the epic poesy and the dramatic, for many reasons he there alleges, ranked above it?

"But setting this defense aside, your argument is almost as strong against the use of rhyme in poems as in plays; for the epic way is everywhere interlaced with dialogue, or discoursive scenes; and therefore you must either grant rhyme to be improper there, which is contrary to your assertion, or admit it into plays by the same title which you have given it to poems. For though tragedy be justly preferred above the other, yet there is a great affinity between them, as may easily be discovered in that definition of a play which Lisideius gave us. The genus of them is the same, a just and lively image of human nature, in its actions, passions, and traverses of fortune: so is the end, namely for the delight and benefit of mankind. The characters and persons are still the same, viz. the greatest of both sorts; only the manner of acquainting us with those actions, passions, and fortunes is different. Tragedy performs it *viva voce*, or by action, in dialogue; wherein it excels the epic poem, which does it chiefly by narration, and therefore is not so lively an image of human nature. However, the agreement betwixt them is such,

---

88. *indignatur enim privatis et prope socco*
    *dignis carminibus narrari caena Thyestae.*
        *Ars poetica*, ll. 90–91.
89. *"effutire leves indigna tragoedia versus"* (*Ibid.*, l. 231).

that if rhyme be proper for one, it must be for the other. Verse, 'tis true, is not the effect of sudden thought; but this hinders not that sudden thought may be represented in verse, since those thoughts are such as must be higher than nature can raise them without premeditation, especially to a continuance of them even out of verse; and consequently you cannot imagine them to have been sudden either in the poet or the actors. A play, as I have said, to be like nature, is to be set above it; as statues which are placed on high are made greater than the life, that they may descend to the sight in their just proportion.

"Perhaps I have insisted too long upon this objection; but the clearing of it will make my stay shorter on the rest. You tell us, Crites, that rhyme appears most unnatural in repartees, or short replies: when he who answers (it being presumed he knew not what the other would say) yet makes up that part of the verse which was left incomplete, and supplies both the sound and measure of it. This, you say, looks rather like the confederacy of two than the answer of one.

"This, I confess, is an objection which is in every one's mouth who loves not rhyme: but suppose, I beseech you, the repartee were made only in blank verse, might not part of the same argument be turned against you? For the measure is as often supplied there as it is in rhyme; the latter half of the hemistich as commonly made up, or a second line subjoined as a reply to the former; which any one leaf in Jonson's plays will sufficiently clear to you. You will often find in the Greek tragedians, and in Seneca, that when a scene grows up into the warmth of repartees (which is the close fighting of it) the latter part of the trimeter is supplied by him who answers; and yet it was never observed as a fault in them by any of the ancient or modern critics. The case is the same in our verse as it was in theirs; rhyme to us being in lieu of quantity to them. But if no latitude is to be allowed a poet, you take from him not only his license of 'daring anything,'[90] but you tie him up in a straiter compass than you would a philosopher. This is indeed 'to cultivate the sterner muses.'[91] You would have him follow

90. *"quidlibet audendi"* (Horace, *Ars poetica*, l. 10).
91. *"Musas colere severiores"* (Martial, Epigrams, IX. xi. 17).

nature, but he must follow her on foot: you have dismounted him from his Pegasus. But, you tell us, this supplying the last half of a verse, or adjoining a whole second to the former, looks more like the design of two than the answer of one. Suppose we acknowledge it: how comes this confederacy to be more displeasing to you than in a dance which is well contrived? You see there the united design of many persons to make up one figure: after they have separated themselves in many petty divisions, they rejoin one by one into a gross: the confederacy is plain amongst them, for chance could never produce anything so beautiful; and yet there is nothing in it that shocks your sight. I acknowledge the hand of art appears in repartee, as of necessity it must in all kinds of verse. But there is also the quick and poignant brevity of it (which is an high imitation of nature in those sudden gusts of passion) to mingle with it; and this, joined with the cadency and sweetness of the rhyme, leaves nothing in the soul of the hearer to desire. 'Tis an art which appears; but it appears only like the shadowings of painture, which being to cause the rounding of it, cannot be absent; but while that is considered, they are lost: so while we attend to the other beauties of the matter, the care and labor of the rhyme is carried from us, or at least drowned in its own sweetness, as bees are sometimes buried in their honey. When a poet has found the repartee, the last perfection he can add to it is to put it into verse. However good the thought may be, however apt the words in which 'tis couched, yet he finds himself at a little unrest, while rhyme is wanting: he cannot leave it till that comes naturally, and then is at ease, and sits down contented.

"From replies, which are the most elevated thoughts of verse, you pass to the most mean ones, those which are common with the lowest of household conversation. In these, you say, the majesty of verse suffers. You instance in the calling of a servant, or commanding a door to be shut, in rhyme. This, Crites, is a good observation of yours, but no argument: for it proves no more but that such thoughts should be waived, as often as may be, by the address of the poet. But suppose they are necessary in the places where he uses them, yet there is no need to put them into rhyme. He may place them in the beginning of a verse, and break it off, as unfit, when so debased, for any other use; or granting the worst, that they require more room than the hemistich will allow, yet still there is a choice to be made of the best words, and least vulgar (provided they be apt) to express such thoughts. Many have blamed rhyme in general for this fault, when the poet with a little care might have redressed it. But they do it with no more justice than if English poesy should be made ridiculous for the sake of the Water Poet's rhymes.[92] Our language is noble, full, and significant; and I know not why he who is master of it may not clothe ordinary things in it as decently as the Latin, if he use the same diligence in his choice of words. 'Delight in words is the source of eloquence.'[93] It was the saying of Julius Caesar, one so curious in his, that none of them can be changed but for a worse. One would think *unlock the door* was a thing as vulgar as could be spoken; and yet Seneca could make it sound high and lofty in his Latin:

*reserate clusos regii postes laris.*[94]

"But I turn from this exception, both because it happens not above twice or thrice in any play that those vulgar thoughts are used; and then too, were there no other apology to be made, yet the necessity of them (which is alike in all kind of writing) may excuse them. Besides that the great eagerness and precipitation with which they are spoken makes us rather mind the substance than the dress; that for which they are spoken, rather than what is spoke. For they are always the effect of some hasty concernment, and something of consequence depends upon them.

"Thus, Crites, I have endeavored to answer your objections; it remains only that I should vindicate an argument for verse, which you have gone about to overthrow. It had formerly been said that the easiness of blank verse renders the poet too luxuriant, but that the labor of rhyme bounds and circumscribes an over-fruitful fancy; the sense there being commonly confined to the couplet, and the words so ordered that the rhyme naturally follows them,

92. An allusion to John Taylor, a Thames waterman, whose doggerel verses enjoyed a great vogue.

93. "*Delectus verborum origo est eloquentiae*" (Cicero, *Brutus*, 72).

94. "Set wide the palace gates" (*Hippolytus*, l. 860).

not they the rhyme. To this you answered that it was no argument to the question in hand; for the dispute was not which way a man may write best, but which is most proper for the subject on which he writes.

"First, give me leave, Sir, to remember you that the argument against which you raised this objection was only secondary: it was built on this hypothesis, that to write in verse was proper for serious plays. Which supposition being granted (as it was briefly made out in that discourse, by showing how verse might be made natural), it asserted that this way of writing was an help to the poet's judgment, by putting bounds to a wild, overflowing fancy. I think, therefore, it will not be hard for me to make good what it was to prove. But you add, that were this let pass, yet he who wants judgment in the liberty of his fancy, may as well show the defect of it when he is confined to verse: for he who has judgment will avoid errors, and he who has it not will commit them in all kinds of writing.

"This argument, as you have taken it from a most acute person, so I confess it carries much weight in it. But by using the word *judgment* here indefinitely, you seem to have put a fallacy upon us. I grant he who has judgment, that is, so profound, so strong, so infallible a judgment, that he needs no helps to keep it always poised and upright, will commit no faults either in rhyme or out of it. And on the other extreme, he who has a judgment so weak and crazed that no helps can correct or amend it, shall write scurvily out of rhyme, and worse in it. But the first of these judgments is no where to be found, and the latter is not fit to write at all. To speak therefore of judgment as it is in the best poets: they who have the greatest proportion of it want other helps than from it within. As for example, you would be loth to say that he who was endued with a sound judgment had no need of history, geography, or moral philosophy, to write correctly. Judgment is indeed the master-workman in a play; but he requires many subordinate hands, many tools to his assistance. And verse I affirm to be one of these: 'tis a rule and line by which he keeps his building compact and even, which otherwise lawless imagination would raise either irregularly or loosely. At least, if the poet commits errors with this help, he would make greater and more without it: 'tis (in short) a slow and painful, but the surest kind of working. Ovid, whom you accuse for luxuriancy in verse, had perhaps been farther guilty of it, had he writ in prose. And for you instance of Ben Jonson who, you say, writ exactly without the help of rhyme, you are to remember 'tis only an aid to luxuriant fancy, which his was not: as he did not want imagination, so none ever said he had much to spare. Neither was verse then refined so much to be an help to that age as it is to ours. Thus, then, the second thoughts being usually the best, as receiving the maturest digestion from judgment, and the last and most mature product of those thoughts being artful and labored verse, it may well be inferred that verse is a great help to a luxuriant fancy; and this is what that argument which you opposed was to evince."

Neander was pursuing this discourse so eagerly that Eugenius had called to him twice or thrice, ere he took notice that the barge stood still, and that they were at the foot of Somerset Stairs, where they had appointed it to land. The company were all sorry to separate so soon, though a great part of the evening was already spent; and stood a while looking back on the water, which the moonbeams played upon, and made it appear like floating quick-silver; at last they went up through a crowd of French people, who were merrily dancing in the open air, and nothing concerned for the noise of guns which had alarmed the town that afternoon. Walking thence together to the Piazze, they parted there; Eugenius and Lisideius to some pleasant appointment they had made, and Crites and Neander to their several lodgings.

FINIS

*Of Dramatic Poesie, An Essay* (London: printed for Henry Herringman, 1668), sigs. A4v–K4v.

# A Defence of
## *An Essay Of Dramatic Poesy*
# Being an Answer to the Preface of
## *The Great Favourite, or The Duke of Lerma*

## Prefixed to the 2d edition of
## *The Indian Emperor*
## (1668)

*The immediate provocation of "A Defence" is Dryden's anger with Sir Robert Howard, and this anger is perhaps the reason why the essay is so revealing. For Dryden is driven not only to defending rhyme but also to defending his most basic professional assumptions against Howard's belle-tristic attitudes. Dryden states unequivocally that pleasing an audience is the chief end of a dramatist, but he also makes clear that plays or poems cannot therefore be judged solely by taste, even the taste of gentlemen. There are rules: dramatic poetry is an imitation of nature, and "if nature be to be imitated, then there is a rule for imitating nature rightly; otherwise there may be an end, and no means conducing to it." The central question for critics and writers is thus the appropriateness of means to ends—otherwise known as decorum—and the classics can help establish these standards of decorum, since literature has always been an imitation of nature and those means which have been found to imitate so as to please centuries of readers must obviously be sound. This argument allows Dryden his usual mediation between the experience of classical literature and criticism and the demands of his own audience.*

The former edition of the *Indian Emperor* being full of faults which had escaped the printer, I have been willing to over-look this second with more care: and though I could not allow myself so much time as was necessary, yet by that little I have done, the press is freed from some gross errors which it had to answer for before. As for the more material faults of writing, which are properly mine, though I see many of them, I want leisure to amend them. 'Tis enough for those who make one poem the business of their lives to leave that correct: yet, excepting Virgil, I never met with any which was so in any language.

But while I was thus employed about this impression, there came to my hands a new printed play called *The Great Favourite, or the Duke of Lerma*; the author of which, a noble and most ingenious person, has done me the favor to make some observations and animadversions upon my *Dramatic Essay*. I must confess he might have better consulted his reputation than by matching himself with so weak an adversary. But if his honor be diminished in the choice of his antagonist, it is sufficiently recompensed in the election of his cause: which being the weaker in all appearance, as combating the received opinions of the best ancient and modern authors, will add to his glory if he overcome, and to the opinion of his generosity, if he be vanquished, since he engages at so great odds; and, so like a cavalier, undertakes the protection of the weaker party. I have only to fear, on my own behalf, that so good a cause as mine may not suffer by my ill management, or weak defense; yet I cannot in honor but take the glove when 'tis offered me; though I am only a champion by succession, and no more able to defend the right of Aristotle and Horace than an infant Dimock[1] to maintain the title of a king.

For my own concernment in the controversy, it is so small that I can easily be contented to be driven from a few notions of dramatic poesy; especially by one who has the reputation of understanding all things: and I might justly make that excuse for my yielding to him which the philosopher made to the Emperor: why should I offer to contend with him who is master of more than twenty legions

1. Since the fourteenth century the Dymokes of Scrivelsby, Lincolnshire, have held the hereditary title of the Sovereign's Champion.

of arts and sciences? But I am forced to fight, and therefore it will be no shame to be overcome.

Yet I am so much his servant as not to meddle with anything which does not concern me in his preface: therefore I leave the good sense and other excellencies of the first twenty lines to be considered by the critics. As for the play of *The Duke of Lerma*, having so much altered and beautified it as he has done, it can justly belong to none but him. Indeed they must be extreme ignorant, as well as envious, who would rob him of that honor; for you see him putting in his claim to it, even in the first two lines:

> Repulse upon repulse, like waves thrown back,
> That slide to hang upon obdurate rocks.[2]

After this, let detraction do its worst; for if this be not his, it deserves to be. For my part, I declare for distributive justice; and from this, and what follows, he certainly deserves *those advantages which he acknowledges to have received from the opinion of sober men.*[3]

In the next place, I must beg leave to observe his great address in courting the reader to his party. For intending to assault all poets, both ancient and modern, he discovers not his whole design at once, but seems only to aim at me, and attacks me on my weakest side, my defense of verse.

To begin with me, he gives me the compellation of *The Author of a Dramatic Essay*; which is a little discourse in dialogue, for the most part borrowed from the observations of others; therefore, that I may not be wanting to him in civility, I return his compliment by calling him *The Author of the Duke of Lerma.*[4]

But (that I may pass over his salute) he takes notice of my great pains to prove rhyme as natural in a serious play, and more effectual than blank verse. Thus indeed I did state the question; but he tells me, *I pursue that which I call natural in a wrong application; for 'tis not the*

2. The opening lines of Howard's play.

3. With the exception of titles, the italicized passages in this essay are quotations from Howard.

4. Dryden's aspersions on Howard's authorship are probably justified, since there is evidence that *The Duke of Lerma* may be an unacknowledged revision of an earlier, lost play.

*question whether rhyme, or not rhyme, be best, or most natural for a serious*
*subject, but what is nearest the nature of that it represents.*

If I have formerly mistaken the question, I must confess my
ignorance so far as to say I continue still in my mistake. But he
ought to have proved that I mistook it; for 'tis yet but *gratis dictum*
[mere assertion]; I still shall think I have gained my point if I
can prove that rhyme is best or most natural for a serious subject.
As for the question as he states it, whether rhyme be nearest the
nature of what it represents, I wonder he should think me so ridiculous as to dispute whether prose or verse be nearest to ordinary
conversation.

It still remains for him to prove his inference: that, since verse is
granted to be more remote than prose from ordinary conversation,
therefore no serious plays ought to be writ in verse; and when he
clearly makes that good, I will acknowledge his victory as absolute
as he can desire it.

The question now is which of us two has mistaken it; and if it
appear I have not, the world will suspect *what gentleman that was,*
*who was allowed to speak twice in Parliament because he had not yet spoken*
*to the question*; and perhaps conclude it to be the same who, as 'tis
reported, maintained a contradiction *in terminis*, in the face of three
hundred persons.

But to return to verse, whether it be natural or not in plays is a
problem which is not demonstrable of either side: 'tis enough for
me that he acknowledges he had rather read good verse than prose:
for if all the enemies of verse will confess as much, I shall not need
to prove that it is natural. I am satisfied if it cause delight; for delight
is the chief, if not the only end of poesy; instruction can be admitted
but in the second place, for poesy only instructs as it delights.
'Tis true that to imitate well is a poet's work; but to affect the soul,
and excite the passions, and, above all, to move admiration (which
is the delight of serious plays), a bare imitation will not serve. The
converse, therefore, which a poet is to imitate, must be heightened
with all the arts and ornaments of poesy; and must be such as,
strictly considered, could never be supposed spoken by any without
premeditation.

As for what he urges, that *a play will still be supposed to be a com-position of several persons speaking* ex tempore; *and that good verses are the hardest things which can be imagined to be so spoken*: I must crave leave to dissent from his opinion, as to the former part of it. For, if I am not deceived, a play is supposed to be the work of the poet, imitating or representing the conversation of several persons: and this I think to be as clear as he thinks the contrary.

But I will be bolder, and do not doubt to make it good, though a paradox, that one great reason why prose is not to be used in serious plays is because it is too near the nature of converse: there may be too great a likeness; as the most skilful painters affirm that there may be too near a resemblance in a picture: to take every lineament and feature is not to make an excellent piece, but to take so much only as will make a beautiful resemblance of the whole: and, with an ingenious flattery of nature, to heighten the beauties of some parts, and hide the deformities of the rest. For so says Horace,

> As with a painting, so with a poem: . . . one prefers the shade, another prefers to be seen in the light, having no fear of the critic's keen judgment. . . . and what cannot be made attractive by his touch, the poet omits.[5]

In *Bartholomew Fair*, or the lowest kind of comedy, that degree of heightening is used which is proper to set off that subject: 'tis true the author was not there to go out of prose, as he does in his higher arguments of comedy, *The Fox* and *Alchemist*; yet he does so raise his matter in that prose as to render it delightful; which he could never have performed, had he only said or done those very things that are daily spoken or practiced in the fair: for then the fair itself would be as full of pleasure to an ingenious person as the play, which we manifestly see it is not. But he hath made an excellent lazar of it; the copy is of price, though the original be

5.  *ut pictura poesis erit, etc . . .*
    *haec amat obscurum, vult haec sub luce videri,*
    *judicis argutum quae non formidat acumen.*
    *. . . et quae*
    *desperat tractata nitescere posse, relinquit.*
    *Ars poetica*, ll. 361–364, 149–150.

vile. You see in *Catiline* and *Sejanus*, where the argument is great,
he sometimes ascends to verse, which shows he thought it not unnatural in serious plays; and had his genius been as proper for
rhyme as it was for humour, or had the age in which he lived
attained to as much knowledge in verse as ours, 'tis probable he
would have adorned those subjects with that kind of writing.[6]

Thus prose, though the rightful prince, yet is by common consent
deposed as too weak for the government of serious plays: and he
failing, there now start up two competitors; one the nearer in blood,
which is blank verse; the other more fit for the ends of government,
which is rhyme. Blank verse is, indeed, the nearer prose, but he is
blemished with the weakness of his predecessor. Rhyme (for I will
deal clearly) has somewhat of the usurper in him, but he is brave,
and generous, and his dominion pleasing. For this reason of delight,
the Ancients (whom I will still believe as wise as those who so
confidently correct them) wrote all their tragedies in verse, though
they knew it most remote from conversation.

But I perceive I am falling into the danger of another rebuke
from my opponent; for when I plead that the Ancients used verse,
I prove not that they would have admitted rhyme, had it then
been written. All I can say is only this, that it seems to have succeeded verse[7] by the general consent of poets in all modern languages; for almost all their serious plays are written in it; which,
though it be no demonstration that therefore they ought to be so,
yet at least the practice first, and then the continuation of it, shows
that it attained the end, which was to please; and if that cannot be
compassed here, I will be the first who shall lay it down. For I
confess my chief endeavors are to delight the age in which I live.
If the humour of this be for low comedy, small accidents, and
raillery, I will force my genius to obey it, though with more reputation I could write in verse. I know I am not so fitted by nature to
write comedy: I want that gaiety of humour which is required to it.
My conversation is slow and dull; my humour saturnine and re-
served: in short, I am none of those who endeavor to break jests
in company, or make repartees. So that those who decry my

6. All the plays Dryden mentions in this paragraph are by Ben Jonson.
7. Dryden must mean blank verse here.

comedies do me no injury, except it be in point of profit: reputation in them is the last thing to which I shall pretend. I beg pardon for entertaining the reader with so ill a subject; but before I quit that argument, which was the cause of this digression, I cannot but take notice how I am corrected for my quotation of Seneca in my defense of plays in verse. My words are these: "Our language is noble, full, and significant; and I know not why he who is master of it may not clothe ordinary things in it as decently as the Latin, if he use the same diligence in his choice of words. One would think *unlock a door* was a thing as vulgar as could be spoken; yet Seneca could make it sound high and lofty in his Latin:

*reserate clusos regii postes laris.*" [8]

But he says of me, "That being filled with the precedents of the Ancients, who writ their plays in verse, I commend the thing, declaring our language to be full, noble, and significant, and charging all defects upon the *ill placing of words*, which I prove by quoting Seneca loftily expressing such an ordinary thing as *shutting a door.*"

Here he manifestly mistakes; for I spoke not of the placing, but of the choice of words; for which I quoted that aphorism of Julius Caesar, *delectus verborum est origo eloquentiae* [delight in words is the source of eloquence]; but *delectus verborum* is no more Latin for the *placing of words*, than *reserate* is Latin for *shut the door*, as he interprets it, which I ignorantly construed *unlock* or *open* it.

He supposes I was highly affected with the sound of those words; and I suppose I may more justly imagine it of him; for if he had not been extremely satisfied with the sound, he would have minded the sense a little better.

But these are now to be no faults; for ten days after his book is published, and that his mistakes are grown so famous that they are come back to him, he sends his *Errata* to be printed, and annexed to his play; and desires that instead of *shutting* you would read *opening*; which, it seems, was the printer's fault. I wonder at his modesty, that he did not rather say it was Seneca's or mine; and

8. "Set wide the palace gates."

that in some authors *reserare* was to *shut* as well as to *open*, as the word *barach*, say the learned, is both to *bless* and *curse*.

Well, since it was the printer, he was a naughty man to commit the same mistake twice in six lines: I warrant you *delectus verborum*, for *placing of words*, was his mistake too, though the author forgot to tell him of it: if it were my book I assure you I should. For those rascals ought to be the proxies of every gentleman author, and to be chastised for him when he is not pleased to own an error. Yet since he has given the *Errata*, I wish he would have enlarged them only a few sheets more, and then he would have spared me the labor of an answer: for this cursed printer is so given to mistakes that there is scarce a sentence in the preface without some false grammar or hard sense in it; which will all be charged upon the poet, because he is so good-natured as to lay but three errors to the printer's account, and to take the rest upon himself, who is better able to support them. But he needs not apprehend that I should strictly examine those little faults, except I am called upon to do it: I shall return therefore to that quotation of Seneca, and answer not to what he writes, but to what he means. I never intended it as an argument, but only as an illustration of what I had said before concerning the election of words; and all he can charge me with is only this, that if Seneca could make an ordinary thing sound well in Latin by the choice of words, the same with the like care might be performed in English: if it cannot, I have committed an error on the right hand, by commending too much the copiousness and well sounding of our language, which I hope my countrymen will pardon me. At least the words which follow in my *Dramatic Essay* will plead somewhat in my behalf; for I say there that this objection happens but seldom in a play; and then too either the meanness of the expression may be avoided, or shut out from the verse by breaking it in the midst.

But I have said too much in the defense of verse; for after all 'tis a very indifferent thing to me whether it obtain or not. I am content hereafter to be ordered by his rule, that is, to write it sometimes because it pleases me, and so much the rather, because he has declared that it pleases him. But he has taken his last farewell of

the Muses, and he has done it civilly, by honoring them with the
name of *his long acquaintances*, which is a compliment they have
scarce deserved from him. For my own part, I bear a share in the
public loss, and how emulous soever I may be of his fame and
reputation, I cannot but give this testimony of his style, that it is
extreme poetical, even in oratory; his thoughts elevated, sometimes
above common apprehension; his notions politic and grave, and
tending to the instruction of princes, and reformation of states;
that they are abundantly interlaced with variety of fancies, tropes,
and figures, which the critics have enviously branded with the name
of obscurity and false grammar.

*Well, he is now fettered in business of more unpleasant nature:* the Muses
have lost him, but the Commonwealth gains by it; the corruption
of a poet is the generation of a statesman.

*He will not venture again into the civil wars of censure, ubi . . . nullos
habitura triumphos*: [9] if he had not told us he had left the Muses, we
might have half suspected it by that word *ubi*, which does not any
way belong to them in that place: the rest of the verse is indeed
Lucan's, but that *ubi*, I will answer for it, is his own. Yet he has
another reason for this disgust of poesy; for he says immediately
after, that *the manner of plays which are now in most esteem is beyond his
power to perform*: to perform the manner of a thing, I confess, is new
English to me. *However, he condemns not the satisfaction of others, but
rather their unnecessary understanding, who, like Sancho Pança's doctor,
prescribe too strictly to our appetites; for*, says he, *in the difference of tragedy
and comedy, and of farce itself, there can be no determination but by the
taste, nor in the manner of their composure.*

We shall see him now as great a critic as he was a poet, and the
reason why he excelled so much in poetry will be evident, for it
will appear to have proceeded from the exactness of his judgment.
*In the difference of tragedy, comedy, and farce itself, there can be no deter-
mination but by the taste.* I will not quarrel with the obscurity of his
phrase, though I justly might; but beg his pardon if I do not
rightly understand him. If he means that there is no essential

9. "where . . . no triumphs are to be won." (Lucan, *Pharsalia*, I. 12). The
"*ubi*" is indeed not to be found in Lucan.

difference betwixt comedy, tragedy, and farce, but what is only made by the people's taste, which distinguishes one of them from the other, that is so manifest an error that I need not lose time to contradict it. Were there neither judge, taste, nor opinion in the world, yet they would differ in their natures; for the action, character, and language of tragedy would still be great and high; that of comedy lower and more familiar; admiration would be the delight of one, and satire of the other.

I have but briefly touched upon these things because, whatever his words are, I can scarce imagine that *he, who is always concerned for the true honor of reason, and would have no spurious issue fathered upon her,* should mean anything so absurd as to affirm *that there is no difference betwixt comedy and tragedy but what is made by the taste only*; unless he would have us understand the comedies of my Lord L., where the first act should be pottages, the second fricasses, &c., and the fifth a *chère entière* [complete fare] of women.

I rather guess he means that betwixt one comedy or tragedy and another there is no other difference but what is made by the liking or disliking of the audience. This is indeed a less error than the former, but yet it is a great one. The liking or disliking of the people gives the play the denomination of good or bad, but does not really make or constitute it such. To please the people ought to be the poet's aim, because plays are made for their delight; but it does not follow that they are always pleased with good plays, or that the plays which please them are always good. The humour of the people is now for comedy, therefore in hope to please them, I write comedies rather than serious plays: and so far their taste prescribes to me: but it does not follow from that reason that comedy is to be preferred before tragedy in its own nature; for that which is so in its own nature cannot be otherwise, as a man cannot but be a rational creature: but the opinion of the people may alter, and in another age, or perhaps in this, serious plays may be set up above comedies.

This I think a sufficient answer; if it be not, he has provided me of an excuse; it seems, in his wisdom, he forsaw my weakness, and has found out this expedient for me, *that it is not necessary for poets to study strict reason, since they are so used to a greater latitude than is allowed by that severe inquisition, that they must infringe their own jurisdiction to profess themselves obliged to argue well.*

I am obliged to him for discovering to me this back door; but I am not yet resolved on my retreat: for I am of opinion that they cannot be good poets who are not accustomed to argue well. False reasonings and colors of speech are the certain marks of one who does not understand the stage; for moral truth is the mistress of the poet as much as of the philosopher: poesy must resemble natural truth, but it must *be* ethical. Indeed the poet dresses truth, and adorns nature, but does not alter them:

Fiction made for delight should resemble truth.[10]

Therefore that is not the best poesy which resembles notions of things that are not to things that are: though the fancy may be great and the words flowing, yet the soul is but half satisfied when there is not truth in the foundation. This is that which makes Virgil be preferred before the rest of poets. In variety of fancy, and sweetness of expression, you see Ovid far above him; for Virgil rejected many of those things which Ovid wrote. *A great wit's great work is to refuse,* as my worthy friend Sir John Berkenhead has ingeniously expressed it: you rarely meet with anything in Virgil but truth, which therefore leaves the strongest impression of pleasure in the soul. This I thought myself obliged to say in behalf of poesy; and to declare, though it be against myself, that when poets do not argue well, the defect is in the workmen, not in the art.

And now I come to the boldest part of his discourse, wherein he attacks not me, but all the Ancients and Moderns; and undermines, as he thinks, the very foundations on which dramatic poesy is built. I could wish he would have declined that envy which must of necessity follow such an undertaking, and contented himself with triumphing over me in my opinions of verse, which I will never hereafter dispute with him; but he must pardon me if I have that veneration for Aristotle, Horace, Ben Jonson, and Corneille, that I dare not serve him in such a cause, and against such heroes, but

10. *"ficta voluptatis causâ sint proxima veris"* (Horace, *Ars poetica*, l. 338).

rather fight under their protection, as Homer reports of little Teucer, who shot the Trojans from under the large buckler of Ajax Telamon:

> Στῆ δ' ἄρ' ὑπ' Αἴαντος σάκεϊ Τελαμωνιάδαω, &c.[11]
> He stood beneath his brother's ample shield;
> And, cover'd there, shot death through all the field.

The words of my noble adversary are these:

*But if we examine the general rules laid down for plays by strict reason, we shall find the errors equally gross; for the great foundation which is laid to build upon is nothing as it is generally stated, as will appear upon the examination of the particulars.*

These particulars in due time shall be examined. In the meanwhile, let us consider what this great foundation is, which he says is nothing, as it is generally stated. I never heard of any other foundation of dramatic poesy than the imitation of nature; neither was there ever pretended any other by the Ancients or Moderns, or me, who endeavor to follow them in that rule. This I have plainly said in my definition of a play: that it is a just and lively image of human nature, &c. Thus the foundation, as it is generally stated, will stand sure, if this definition of a play be true; if it be not, he ought to have made his exception against it, by proving that a play is not an imitation of nature, but somewhat else which he is pleased to think it.

But 'tis very plain that he has mistaken the foundation for that which is built upon it, though not immediately; for the direct and immediate consequence is this: if nature be to be imitated, then there is a rule for imitating nature rightly; otherwise there may be an end, and no means conducing to it. Hitherto I have proceeded by demonstration; but as our divines, when they have proved a Deity because there is order, and have inferred that this Deity ought to be worshipped, differ afterwards in the manner of the worship; so having laid down that nature is to be imitated, and that proposition proving the next, that then there are means which conduce to the imitating of nature, I dare proceed no further positively; but have only laid down some opinions of the Ancients

11. *Iliad*, viii. 267.

and Moderns, and of my own, as means which they used, and which I thought probable for the attaining of that end. Those means are the same which my antagonist calls the foundations, how properly the world may judge; and to prove that this is his meaning, he clears it immediately to you by enumerating those rules or propositions against which he makes his particular exceptions; as namely, those of time and place, in these words: *First, we are told the plot should not be so ridiculously contrived as to crowd two several countries into one stage; secondly, to cramp the accidents of many years or days into the representation of two hours and a half; and, lastly, a conclusion drawn, that the only remaining dispute is concerning time, whether it should be contained in twelve or twenty-four hours; and the place to be limited to that spot of ground where the play is supposed to begin: and this is called nearest nature; for that is concluded most natural which is most probable, and nearest to that which it presents.*

Thus he has only made a small mistake of the means conducing to the end for the end itself, and of the superstructure for the foundation; but he proceeds: *to show therefore upon what ill grounds they dictate laws for dramatic poesy*, &c. He is here pleased to charge me with being magisterial, as he has done in many other places of his preface. Therefore, in vindication of myself, I must crave leave to say that my whole discourse was sceptical, according to that way of reasoning which was used by Socrates, Plato, and all the Academics of old, which Tully and the best of the Ancients followed, and which is imitated by the modest inquisitions of the Royal Society.[12] That it is so, not only the name will show, which is *An Essay*, but the frame and composition of the work. You see it is a dialogue sustained by persons of several opinions, all of them left doubtful, to be determined by the readers in general; and more particularly deferred to the accurate judgment of my Lord Buckhurst, to whom I made a dedication of my book. These are my words in my epistle, speaking of the persons whom I introduced in my dialogue: "'Tis true they differed in their opinions, as 'tis

12. Dryden was an early member of the Royal Society, though he was soon dropped for failure to attend meetings. In this passage Dryden apparently sees the scientific skepticism of the Royal Society as a descendant of Socratic skepticism, a skepticism with which he endeavors to ally his own procedure.

probable they would; neither do I take upon me to reconcile, but to relate them, leaving your Lordship to decide it in favor of that part which you shall judge most reasonable." And after that, in my advertisement to the reader, I said this: "The drift of the ensuing discourse is chiefly to vindicate the honor of our English writers from the censure of those who unjustly prefer the French before them. This I intimate, lest any should think me so exceeding vain as to teach others an art which they understand much better than myself." But this is more than necessary to clear my modesty in that point: and I am very confident that there is scarce any man who has lost so much time as to read that trifle, but will be my compurgator as to that arrogance whereof I am accused. The truth is, if I had been naturally guilty of so much vanity as to dictate my opinions, yet I do not find that the character of a positive or self-conceited person is of such advantage to any in this age that I should labor to be publicly admitted of that order.

But I am not now to defend my own cause, when that of all the Ancients and Moderns is in question: for this gentleman who accuses me of arrogance has taken a course not to be taxed with the other extreme of modesty. Those propositions which are laid down in my discourse, as helps to the better imitation of nature, are not mine (as I have said), nor were ever pretended so to be, but derived from the authority of Aristotle and Horace, and from the rules and examples of Ben Jonson and Corneille. These are the men with whom properly he contends, and against *whom he will endeavor to make it evident, that there is no such thing as what they all pretend.*

His argument against the unities of place and time is this: *that 'tis as impossible for one stage to present two rooms or houses truly, as two countries or kingdoms; and as impossible that five hours or twenty-four hours should be two hours, as that a thousand hours or years should be less than what they are, or the greatest part of time to be comprehended in the less: for all of them being impossible, they are none of them nearest the truth or nature of what they present; for impossibilities are all equal, and admit of no degree.*

This argument is so scattered into parts that it can scarce be united into a syllogism; yet, in obedience to him, *I will abbreviate* and comprehend as much of it as I can in few words, that my answer to it may be more perspicuous. I conceive his meaning to be what follows, as to the unity of place (if I mistake, I beg his pardon, professing it is not out of any design to play the *argumentative poet*). If one stage cannot properly present two rooms or houses, much less two countries or kingdoms, then there can be no unity of place: but one stage cannot properly perform this; therefore there can be no unity of place.

I plainly deny his minor proposition; the force of which, if I mistake not, depends on this, that the stage being one place cannot be two. This indeed is as great a secret as that we are all mortal; but to requite it with another, I must crave leave to tell him that though the stage cannot be two places, yet it may properly represent them successively, or at several times. His argument is indeed no more than a mere fallacy, which will evidently appear when we distinguish place, as it relates to plays, into real and imaginary. The real place is that theater or piece of ground on which the play is acted. The imaginary, that house, town, or country where the action of the *drama* is supposed to be; or, more plainly, where the scene of the play is laid. Let us now apply this to that Herculean argument, *which if strictly and duly weighed, is to make it evident that there is no such thing as what they all pretend.* 'Tis impossible, he says, for one stage to present two rooms or houses: I answer, 'tis neither impossible, nor improper, for one real place to represent two or more imaginary places, so it be done successively, which in other words is no more than this: that the imagination of the audience, aided by the words of the poet and painted scenes, may suppose the stage to be sometimes one place, sometimes another, now a garden, or wood, and immediately a camp: which I appeal to every man's imagination, if it be not true. Neither the Ancients nor Moderns, as much fools as he is pleased to think them, ever asserted that they could make one place two; but they might hope, by the good leave of this author, that the change of a scene might lead the imagination to suppose the place altered: so that he cannot fasten those absurdities upon this scene of a play, or imaginary place of action, that it is one place and yet two.

And this being so clearly proved, that 'tis past any show of reasonable denial, it will not be hard to destroy that other part of his argument which depends upon it, namely, that 'tis as impossible for a stage to represent two rooms or houses, as two countries or kingdoms: for his reason is already overthrown, which was because both were alike impossible. This is manifestly otherwise: for 'tis proved that a stage may properly represent two rooms or houses; for the imagination being judge of what is represented, will in reason be less shocked with the appearance of two rooms in the same house, or two houses in the same city, than with two distant cities in the same country, or two remote countries in the same universe. Imagination in a man, or reasonable creature, is supposed to participate of reason, and when that governs, as it does in the belief of fiction, reason is not destroyed, but misled, or blinded: that can prescribe to the reason, during the time of the representation, somewhat like a weak belief of what it sees and hears; and reason suffers itself to be so hoodwinked, that it may better enjoy the pleasures of the fiction: but it is never so wholly made a captive as to be drawn headlong into a persuasion of those things which are most remote from probability: 'tis in that case a free-born subject, not a slave; it will contribute willingly its assent, as far as it sees convenient, but will not be forced. Now there is a greater vicinity in nature betwixt two rooms than betwixt two houses; betwixt two houses than betwixt two cities; and so of the rest: reason therefore can sooner be led by imagination to step from one room into another than to walk to two distant houses, and yet rather to go thither than to fly like a witch through the air, and be hurried from one region to another. Fancy and reason go hand in hand; the first cannot leave the last behind: and though fancy, when it sees the wide gulf, would venture over, as the nimbler, yet it is withheld by reason, which will refuse to take the leap when the distance over it appears too large. If Ben Jonson himself will remove the scene from Rome into Tuscany in the same act, and from thence return to Rome in the scene which immediately follows, reason will consider there is no proportionable allowance of time to perform the journey, and therefore will choose to stay at home. So, then, the less change of place there is, the less time is taken up in transporting the persons of the drama, with analogy to reason; and in that analogy, or resemblance of fiction to truth, consists the excellency of the play.

For what else concerns the unity of place, I have already given my opinion of it in my *Essay*, that there is a latitude to be allowed to it, as several places in the same town or city, or places adjacent to each other in the same country; which may all be comprehended under the larger denomination of one place; yet with this restriction, that the nearer and fewer those imaginary places are, the greater resemblance they will have to truth; and reason, which cannot make them one, will be more easily led to suppose so.

What has been said of the unity of place may easily be applied to that of time: I grant it to be impossible that the greater part of time should be comprehended in the less, that twenty-four hours should be crowded into three: but there is no necessity of that supposition; for as *place*, so *time* relating to a play is either imaginary or real: the real is comprehended in those three hours, more or less, in the space of which the play is represented; the imaginary is that which is supposed to be taken up in the representation, as twenty-four hours more or less. Now no man ever could suppose that twenty-four real hours could be included in the space of three; but where is the absurdity of affirming that the feigned business of twenty-four imagined hours may not more naturally be represented in the compass of three real hours, than the like feigned business of twenty-four years in the same proportion of real time? For the proportions are always real, and much nearer, by his permission, of twenty-four to three, than of four thousand to it.

I am almost fearful of illustrating anything by similitude, lest he should confute it for an argument; yet I think the comparison of a glass will discover very aptly the fallacy of his argument, both concerning time and place. The strength of his reason depends on this, that the less cannot comprehend the greater. I have already answered that we need not suppose it does; I say not that the less can comprehend the greater, but only that it may represent it; as in a glass or mirror of half-a-yard diameter, a whole room and many persons in it may be seen at once: not that it can comprehend that room or those persons, but that it represents them to the sight.

But the author of the *Duke of Lerma* is to be excused for his declaring against the unity of time; for, if I be not much mistaken, he is an interested person; the time of that play taking up so many years as the favor of the Duke of Lerma continued; nay, the second and third act including all the time of his prosperity, which was a great part of the reign of Philip the Third: for in the beginning of the second act he was not yet a favorite, and before the end of the third was in disgrace. I say not this with the least design of limiting the stage too servilely to twenty-four hours, however he be pleased to tax me with dogmatizing on that point. In my dialogue, as I before hinted, several persons maintained their several opinions: one of them, indeed, who supported the cause of the French poesy, said how strict they were in that particular; but he who answered in behalf of our nation was willing to give more latitude to the rule, and cites the words of Corneille himself, complaining against the severity of it, and observing what beauties it banished from the stage, *pag.* 44 of my *Essay*. In few words, my own opinion is this (and I willingly submit it to my adversary, when he will please impartially to consider it) that the imaginary time of every play ought to be contrived into as narrow a compass as the nature of the plot, the quality of the persons, and variety of accidents will allow. In comedy, I would not exceed twenty-four or thirty hours; for the plot, accidents, and persons of comedy are small, and may be naturally turned in a little compass: but in tragedy the design is weighty, and the persons great; therefore there will naturally be required a greater space of time in which to move them. And this, though Ben Jonson has not told us, yet 'tis manifestly his opinion: for you see that to his comedies he allows generally but twenty-four hours; to his two tragedies, *Sejanus* and *Catiline,* a much larger time, though he draws both of them into as narrow a compass as he can. For he shows you only the latter end of Sejanus his favor, and the conspiracy of Catiline already ripe, and just breaking out into action.

But as it is an error, on the one side, to make too great a disproportion betwixt the imaginary time of the play, and the real time of its representation; so, on the other side, 'tis an oversight to compress the accidents of a play into a narrower compass than that in which they could naturally be produced. Of this last error the French are seldom guilty, because the thinness of their plots prevents them from it; but few Englishmen, except Ben Jonson, have ever made a plot with variety of design in it included in twenty-four hours which was altogether natural. For this reason, I prefer the *Silent Woman* before all other plays, I think justly, as I do its author in judgment above all other poets. Yet, of the two, I think that error the most pardonable, which in too strait a compass crowds together many accidents, since it produces more variety, and consequently more pleasure to the audience; and because the nearness of proportion betwixt the imaginary and real time does speciously cover the compression of the accidents.

Thus I have endeavored to answer the meaning of his argument; for as he drew it, I humbly conceive that it was none: as will appear by his proposition, and the proof of it. His proposition was this:

*If strictly and duly weighed, 'tis as impossible for one stage to present two rooms or houses, as two countries or kingdoms, &c.* And his proof this: *For all being impossible, they are none of them nearest the truth or nature of what they present.*

Here you see, instead of proof or reason, there is only a *petitio principii* [fallacy of begging the question]. For, in plain words, his sense is this: two things are as impossible as one another, because they are both equally impossible; but he takes those two things to be granted as impossible which he ought to have proved such before he had proceeded to prove them equally impossible; he should have made out first that it was impossible for one stage to represent two houses, and then have gone forward to prove that it was as equally impossible for a stage to present two houses as two countries.

After all this, the very absurdity to which he would reduce me is none at all: for he only drives at this, that if his argument be true, I must then acknowledge that there are degrees in impossibilities, which I easily grant him without dispute: and, if I mistake not, Aristotle and the School are of my opinion. For there are some things which are absolutely impossible, and others which are only so *ex parte* [from one point of view]; as 'tis absolutely impossible for a thing *to be* and *not be* at the same time: but for a stone to move naturally upward is only impossible *ex parte materiae*; but it is not impossible for the First Mover to alter the nature of it.

His last assault, like that of a Frenchman, is most feeble; for whereas I have observed that none have been violent against verse, but such only as have not attempted it, or have succeeded ill in their attempt, he will needs, according to his usual custom, improve my observation to an argument that he might have the glory to confute it. But I lay my observation at his feet, as I do my pen, which I have often employed willingly in his deserved commendations, and now most unwillingly against his judgment. For his person and parts, I honor them as much as any man living, and have had so many particular obligations to him that I should be very ungrateful if I did not acknowledge them to the world. But I gave not the first occasion of this difference in opinions. In my epistle dedicatory before my *Rival Ladies*, I had said somewhat in behalf of verse which he was pleased to answer in his preface to his plays: that occasioned my reply in my *Essay*; and that reply begot this rejoinder of his, in his preface to the *Duke of Lerma*. But as I was the last who took up arms, I will be the first to lay them down. For what I have here written, I submit it wholly to him; and if I do not hereafter answer what may be objected against this paper, I hope the world will not impute it to any other reason than only the due respect which I have for so noble an opponent.

"A Defence of an Essay of Dramatique Poesie, being an Answer to the Preface of *The Great Favourite, or the Duke of Lerma*." In John Dryden, *The Indian Emperour, Or, The Conquest of Mexico by the Spaniards* (2d ed.; London: printed for H. Herringman, 1668), sigs. A2–b3.

□                                                                                     □

# Preface to
# *An Evening's Love: or The Mock Astrologer*
# (1671)

*The preface to* An Evening's Love *constitutes Dryden's most extensive discussion of comedy. Like his other essays, it is born of controversy, in this case a quarrel with Thomas Shadwell, the poet and playwright whom Dryden was later to pillory in* MacFlecknoe. *Shadwell wrote Jonsonian comedies of humour, and in his critical prefaces, some of which attacked Dryden directly, he argued, on Jonson's authority, that moral plots and characterizations of humours were far more essential to true comedy than verbal wit. In the preface Dryden answers Shadwell's argument in two ways, both of them indicative of his creative and critical temperament. In the first place, he questions Jonson's or any man's absolute authority in literary matters:* "Why," *he asks,* "should there be an* ipse dixit [*the master himself has spoken*] *in our poetry anymore than there is in our philosophy?" And second, he justifies the importance of verbal wit in comedy by insisting, as he always did, upon the primacy of the graces of writing themselves in giving pleasure to an audience:* ". . . in general, the employment of a poet is like that of a curious gunsmith or watchmaker: the iron or silver is not his own; but they are the least part of that which gives the value: the price lies wholly in the workmanship."

I had thought, Reader, in this preface to have written somewhat concerning the difference betwixt the plays of our age and those of our predecessors on the English stage: to have shown in what parts of dramatic poesy we were excelled by Ben Jonson, I mean humour and contrivance of comedy; and in what we may justly claim precedence of Shakespeare and Fletcher, namely in heroic plays. But this design I have waived on second considerations; at least deferred it till I publish the *Conquest of Granada*, where the discourse will be more proper. I had also prepared to treat of the improvement of our language since Fletcher's and Jonson's days, and consequently of our refining the courtship, raillery, and conversation of plays: but as I am willing to decline that envy which I should draw on myself from some old opiniatre[1] judges of the stage; so likewise I am pressed in time so much that I have not leisure, at present, to go through with it.

Neither, indeed, do I value a reputation gained from comedy so far as to concern myself about it any more than I needs must in my own defense: for I think it, in its own nature, inferior to all sorts of dramatic writing. Low comedy especially requires, on the writer's part, much of conversation with the vulgar: and much of ill nature in the observation of their follies. But let all men please themselves according to their several tastes: that which is not pleasant to me may be to others who judge better; and, to prevent an accusation from my enemies, I am sometimes ready to imagine that my disgust of low comedy proceeds not so much from my judgment as from my temper; which is the reason why I so seldom write it; and that when I succeed in it (I mean so far as to please the audience), yet I am nothing satisfied with what I have done; but am often vexed to hear the people laugh, and clap, as they perpetually do, where I intended 'em no jest; while they let pass the better things without taking notice of them. Yet even this confirms me in my opinion of slighting popular applause, and of contemning that approbation which those very people give, equally with me, to the zany of a mountebank; or to the appearance of an antic on the theater, without wit on the poet's part, or any occasion of laughter from the actor besides the ridiculousness of his habit and his grimaces.

But I have descended, before I was aware, from comedy to farce; which consists principally of grimaces. That I admire not any comedy equally with tragedy is, perhaps, from the sullenness of my humour; but that I detest those farces which are now the most frequent entertainments of the stage, I am sure I have reason on my

1. Stubborn.

side. Comedy consists, though of low persons, yet of natural actions and characters; I mean such humours, adventures, and designs as are to be found and met with in the world. Farce, on the other side, consists of forced humours and unnatural events. Comedy presents us with the imperfections of human nature. Farce entertains us with what is monstrous and chimerical: the one causes laughter in those who can judge of men and manners, by the lively representation of their folly or corruption; the other produces the same effect in those who can judge of neither, and that only by its extravagances. The first works on the judgment and fancy; the latter on the fancy only: there is more of satisfaction in the former kind of laughter, and in the latter more of scorn. But how it happens that an impossible adventure should cause our mirth, I cannot so easily imagine. Something there may be in the oddness of it, because on the stage it is the common effect of things unexpected to surprise us into a delight: and that is to be ascribed to the strange appetite, as I may call it, of the fancy; which, like that of a longing woman, often runs out into the most extravagant desires; and is better satisfied sometimes with loam, or with the rinds of trees, than with the wholesome nourishments of life. In short, there is the same difference betwixt farce and comedy as betwixt an empiric[2] and a true physician: both of them may attain their ends; but what the one performs by hazard, the other does by skill. And as the artist is often unsuccessful while the mountebank succeeds; so farces more commonly take the people than comedies. For to write unnatural things is the most probable way of pleasing them, who understand not nature. And a true poet often misses of applause because he cannot debase himself to write so ill as to please his audience.

After all, it is to be acknowledged that most of those comedies which have been lately written have been allied too much to farce; and this must of necessity fall out till we forbear the translation of French plays: for their poets, wanting judgment to make or to maintain true characters, strive to cover their defects with ridiculous figures and grimaces. While I say this, I accuse myself as well as others: and this very play would rise up in judgment against me, if I would defend all things I have written to be natural: but I confess I have given too much to the people in it, and am ashamed for them as

2. A quack.

well as for myself, that I have pleased them at so cheap a rate.
Not that there is anything here which I would not defend to an
ill-natured judge (for I despise their censures, who I am sure
would write worse on the same subject): but because I love to
deal clearly and plainly, and to speak of my own faults with more
criticism than I would of another poet's. Yet I think it no vanity to
say that this comedy has as much of entertainment in it as many
other which have been lately written: and, if I find my own errors
in it, I am able at the same time to arraign all my contemporaries
for greater. As I pretend not that I can write humour, so none of
them can reasonably pretend to have written it as they ought.
Jonson was the only man of all ages and nations who has performed
it well, and that but in three or four of his comedies: the rest are
but a "mess repeatedly served up";[3] the same humours a little varied
and written worse. Neither was it more allowable in him than it
is in our present poets to represent the follies of particular persons;
of which many have accused him. "To spare individuals and speak
of vices"[4] is the rule of plays. And Horace tells you that the Old
Comedy amongst the Grecians was silenced for the too great
liberties of the poets:

> its freedom turned to license and excess which deserved to be checked
> by law; the law was passed, and the right to libel being gone, the
> chorus, to its shame, became mute.[5]

Of which he gives you the reason in another place: where, having
given the precept,

> that they should not give way to bawdy and shameless jokes,

he immediately subjoins,

> for men of rank, birth and fortune are offended by them.[6]

3. *"crambe bis cocte"* (an adaptation of a phrase in Juvenal, *Satires*, VII. 154).
4. *"Parcere personis, dicere de vitiis"* (a Latin proverbial tag).
5. *in vitium libertas excidit et vim*
   *dignam lege regi: lex est accepta, chorusque*
   *turpiter obticuit, sublato jure nocendi.*
               *Ars poetica*, ll. 282–284.
6. *neve immunda crepent, ignominiosaque dicta*
   *offenduntur enim quibus est equus, et pater, et res.*
               *Ibid.*, ll. 247–248.

But Ben Jonson is to be admired for many excellencies; and can be taxed with fewer failings than any English poet. I know I have been accused as an enemy of his writings; but without any other reason than that I do not admire him blindly, and without looking into his imperfections. For why should he only be exempted from those frailties from which Homer and Virgil are not free? Or why should there be any *ipse dixit* in our poetry, any more than there is in our philosophy? I admire and applaud him where I ought: those who do more do but value themselves in their admiration of him; and, by telling you they extol Ben Jonson's way, would insinuate to you that they can practice it. For my part, I declare that I want judgment to imitate him; and should think it a great impudence in myself to attempt it. To make men appear pleasantly ridiculous on the stage was, as I have said, his talent; and in this he needed not the acumen of wit, but that of judgment. For the characters and representations of folly are only the effects of observation; and observation is an effect of judgment. Some ingenious men, for whom I have a particular esteem, have thought I have much injured Ben Jonson when I have not allowed his wit to be extraordinary: but they confound the notion of what is witty with what is pleasant. That Ben Jonson's plays were pleasant, he must want reason who denies: but the pleasantness was not properly wit, or the sharpness of conceit, but the natural imitation of folly: which I confess to be excellent in its kind, but not to be of that kind which they pretend. Yet if we will believe Quintilian in his chapter "On Exciting Laughter," he gives his opinion of both in these following words: "it is easy to ridicule folly, for folly is ridiculous in itself, but something of our own makes the joke have grace."[7] And some perhaps would be apt to say of Jonson as it was said of Demosthenes: "not that he disliked jokes, but that he lacked the power to make them."[8]

I will not deny but that I approve most the mixed way of comedy; that which is neither all wit, nor all humour, but the result of both. Neither so little of humour as Fletcher shows, nor so little of love and wit as Jonson; neither all cheat, with which the best plays of the

7. *De movendo risu:* "*stulta reprehendere facillimum est; nam per se sunt ridicula: et a derisu non procul abest risus: sed rem urbanum facit aliqua ex nobis adjectio*" (*Institutio oratoria*, VI. iii. 2).

8. "*non displicuisse illi jocos, sed non contigisse*" (*Ibid.*, VI. iii. 2).

one are filled, nor all adventure, which is the common practice of the other. I would have the characters well chosen, and kept distant from interfering with each other; which is more than Fletcher or Shakespeare did: but I would have more of the "urbanity, grace, piquancy, elegance," [9] and the rest which Quintilian reckons up as the ornaments of wit; and these are extremely wanting in Ben Jonson. As for repartee in particular; as it is the very soul of conversation, so it is the greatest grace of comedy, where it is proper to the characters. There may be much of acuteness in a thing well said; but there is more in a quick reply: "for wit always looks more graceful in reply than in attack." [10] Of one thing I am sure, that no man ever will decry wit but he who despairs of it himself; and who has no other quarrel to it but that which the fox had to the grapes. Yet, as Mr. Cowley (who had a greater portion of it than any man I know) tells us in his character of wit, rather than all wit let there be none. [11] I think there's no folly so great in any poet of our age as the superfluity and waste of wit was in some of our predecessors: particularly we may say of Fletcher and of Shakespeare what was said of Ovid, "in all his wit you will find it easier to reject than to add." [12] The contrary of which was true in Virgil, and our incomparable Jonson.

Some enemies of repartee have observed to us that there is a great latitude in their characters which are made to speak it: and that it is easier to write wit than humour; because, in the characters of humour, the poet is confined to make the person speak what is only proper to it. Whereas all kind of wit is proper in the character of a witty person. But, by their favor, there are as different characters in wit as in folly. Neither is all kind of wit proper in the mouth of every ingenious person. A witty coward and a witty brave must speak differently. Falstaff and the Liar speak not like Don John in the *Chances*, and Valentine in *Wit without Money*.[13] And Jonson's Truewit in the *Silent Woman* is a character different from all of them.

9. *"urbana, venusta, salsa, faceta" (Ibid.,* VI. iii. 17–20).

10. *"sunt enim longe venustiora omnia in respondendo quam in provocando" (Ibid.,* VI. iii. 13).

11. See Abraham Cowley, "Ode: Of Wit," ll. 35–36.

12. *"in omni ejus ingenio, facilius quod rejici, quam quod adjici potest, invenies"* (Quintilian, *Institutio oratoria,* VI. iii. 5).

13. Both comedies by John Fletcher.

Yet it appears that this one character of wit was more difficult to the author than all his images of humour in the play: for those he could describe and manage from his observations of men; this he has taken, at least a part of it, from books: witness the speeches in the first act, translated *verbatim* out of Ovid *De arte amandi*; to omit what afterwards he borrowed from the sixth satire of Juvenal against women.

However, if I should grant that there were a greater latitude in characters of wit than in those of humour; yet that latitude would be of small advantage to such poets who have too narrow an imagination to write it. And to entertain an audience perpetually with humour is to carry them from the conversation of gentlemen, and treat them with the follies and extravagances of Bedlam.

I find I have launched out farther than I intended in the beginning of this preface. And that, in the heat of writing, I have touched at something which I thought to have avoided. 'Tis time now to draw homeward: and to think rather of defending myself than assaulting others. I have already acknowledged that this play is far from perfect: but I do not think myself obliged to discover the imperfections of it to my adversaries, any more than a guilty person is bound to accuse himself before his judges. 'Tis charged upon me that I make debauched persons (such as, they say, my Astrologer and Gamester are) my protagonists, or the chief persons of the drama; and that I make them happy in the conclusion of my play; against the law of comedy, which is to reward virtue and punish vice. I answer first, that I know no such law to have been constantly observed in comedy, either by the ancient or modern poets. Chaerea is made happy in the *Eunuch*, after having deflowered a virgin; and Terence generally does the same through all his plays, where you perpetually see not only debauched young men enjoy their mistresses, but even the courtesans themselves rewarded and honored in the catastrophe. The same may be observed in Plautus almost everywhere. Ben Jonson himself, after whom I may be proud to err, has given me more than once the example of it. That in the *Alchemist* is notorious, where Face, after having contrived and carried on the great cozenage of the play, and continued in it without repentance to the last, is not only forgiven by his master, but enriched by his consent with the spoils of those whom he had cheated. And, which is more, his master himself, a grave man and a widower, is introduced taking his man's counsel, debauching the widow first, in hope to marry her afterward. In the *Silent Woman*, Dauphine (who, with the other two gentlemen, is of the same character with my Celadon in the *Maiden Queen*, and with Wildblood in this) professes himself in love with all the Collegiate Ladies: and they likewise are all of the same character with each other, excepting only Madam Otter, who has something singular: yet this naughty Dauphine is crowned in the end with the possession of his uncle's estate, and with the hopes of enjoying all his mistresses; and his friend Mr. Truewit (the best character of a gentleman which Ben Jonson ever made) is not ashamed to pimp for him. As for Beaumont and Fletcher, I need not allege examples out of them; for that were to quote almost all their comedies.

But now it will be objected that I patronize vice by the authority of former poets, and extenuate my own faults by recrimination. I answer that, as I defend myself by their example, so that example I defend by reason, and by the end of all dramatic poesy. In the first place, therefore, give me leave to show you their mistake who have accused me. They have not distinguished, as they ought, betwixt the rules of tragedy and comedy. In tragedy, where the actions and persons are great, and the crimes horrid, the laws of justice are more strictly to be observed; and examples of punishments to be made to deter mankind from the pursuit of vice. Faults of this kind have been rare amongst the ancient poets: for they have punished in Oedipus, and in his posterity, the sin which he knew not he had committed. Medea is the only example I remember at present who escapes from punishment after murder. Thus tragedy fulfils one great part of its institution: which is, by example, to instruct. But in comedy it is not so; for the chief end of it is divertisement and delight: and that so much, that it is disputed, I think, by Heinsius, before Horace his *Art of Poetry*, whether instruction be any part of its employment.[14] At least I am sure it can be but its secondary end: for the business of the poet is to make

14. Heinsius had made no such claim. Renaissance critics had normally placed equal stress upon both parts of the Horatian formula, teaching and delighting, and Dryden's emphasis upon delighting an audience is a reflection of his own dramatic experience.

you laugh: when he writes humour, he makes folly ridiculous;
when wit, he moves you, if not always to laughter, yet to a pleasure
that is more noble. And if he works a cure on folly, and the small
imperfections in mankind, by exposing them to public view, that
cure is not performed by an immediate operation. For it works
first on the ill nature of the audience; they are moved to laugh by
the representation of deformity; and the shame of that laughter
teaches us to amend what is ridiculous in our manners. This being,
then, established, that the first end of comedy is delight, and instruction only the second, it may reasonably be inferred that comedy
is not so much obliged to the punishment of faults which it represents, as tragedy. For the persons in comedy are of a lower quality,
the action is little, and the faults and vices are but the sallies of
youth, and the frailties of human nature, and not premeditated
crimes: such to which all men are obnoxious, not such as are attempted only by few, and those abandoned to all sense of virtue: such as
move pity and commiseration, not detestation and horror; such,
in short, as may be forgiven, not such as must of necessity be
punished. But, lest any man should think that I write this to make
libertinism amiable, or that I cared not to debase the end and institution of comedy so I might thereby maintain my own errors, and
those of better poets, I must further declare, both for them and for
myself, that we make not vicious persons happy, but only as Heaven
makes sinners so; that is, by reclaiming them first from vice. For so
'tis to be supposed they are, when they resolve to marry; for then
enjoying what they desire in one, they cease to pursue the love of
many. So Chaerea is made happy by Terence, in marrying her
whom he had deflowered: and so are Wildblood and the Astrologer
in this play.

There is another crime with which I am charged, at which I
am yet much less concerned, because it does not relate to my manners, as the former did, but only to my reputation as a poet: a name
of which I assure the reader I am nothing proud; and therefore
cannot be very solicitous to defend it. I am taxed with stealing all
my plays, and that by some who should be the last men from whom
I would steal any part of 'em. There is one answer which I will not

make; but it has been made for me by him to whose grace and patronage I owe all things,

all the hopes and prospects of scholars depend on Caesar alone,[15]

and without whose command they should no longer be troubled with anything of mine, that he only desired that they who accused me of theft would always steal him plays like mine. But though I have reason to be proud of this defense, yet I should waive it, because I have a worse opinion of my own comedies than any of my enemies can have. 'Tis true that, wherever I have liked any story in a romance, novel, or foreign play, I have made no difficulty, nor ever shall, to take the foundation of it, to build it up, and to make it proper for the English stage. And I will be so vain to say it has lost nothing in my hands: but it always cost me so much trouble to heighten it for our theater (which is incomparably more curious in all the ornaments of dramatic poesy than the French or Spanish), that when I had finished my play, it was like the hulk of Sir Francis Drake, so strangely altered that there scarce remained any plank of the timber which first built it. To witness this, I need go no farther than this play: it was first Spanish, and called *El astrologo fingido*; then made French by the younger Corneille; and is now translated into English, and in print, under the name of the *Feigned Astrologer*.[16] What I have performed in this will best appear by comparing it with those: you will see that I have rejected some adventures which I judged were not divertising; that I have heightened those which I have chosen, and that I have added others which were neither in the French nor Spanish. And besides, you will easily discover that the walk of the Astrologer is the least considerable in my play: for the design of it turns more on the parts of Wildblood and Jacinta, who are the chief persons in it. I have farther to add that I seldom use the wit and language of any romance or play which I undertake to alter: because my own

15. "*et spes et ratio studiorum in Caesare tantum*" (Juvenal, *Satires*, VII. 1).

16. Thomas Corneille's version was called *Le feint astrologue* (1651) and was anonymously adapted into English as *The Feigned Astrologer* (1668). The original Spanish comedy was by Calderón.

invention (as bad as it is) can furnish me with nothing so dull as what is there. Those who have called Virgil, Terence, and Tasso plagiaries (though they much injured them), had yet a better color for their accusation; for Virgil has evidently translated Theocritus, Hesiod, and Homer, in many places; besides what he has taken from Ennius in his own language. Terence was not only known to translate Menander (which he avows also in his prologues), but was said also to be helped in those translations by Scipio the African and Laelius. And Tasso, the most excellent of modern poets, and whom I reverence next to Virgil, has taken both from Homer many admirable things which were left untouched by Virgil, and from Virgil himself where Homer could not furnish him. Yet the bodies of Virgil's and Tasso's poems were their own; and so are all the ornaments of language and elocution in them. The same (if there were anything commendable in this play) I could say for it. But I will come nearer to our own countrymen. Most of Shakespeare's plays, I mean the stories of them, are to be found in the *Hecatommithi* or *Hundred Novels* of Cinthio. I have myself read in his Italian that of *Romeo and Juliet*, the *Moor of Venice*, and many others of them.[17] Beaumont and Fletcher had most of theirs from Spanish novels: witness the *Chances*, the *Spanish Curate*, *Rule a Wife and Have a Wife*, the *Little French Lawyer*, and so many others of them as compose the greatest part of their volume in folio. Ben Jonson, indeed, has designed his plots himself; but no man has borrowed so much from the Ancients as he has done: and he did well in it, for he has thereby beautified our language.

But these little critics do not well consider what is the work of a poet, and what the graces of a poem. The story is the least part of either: I mean the foundation of it, before it is modeled by the art of him who writes it; who forms it with more care, by exposing only the beautiful parts of it to view, than a skilful lapidary sets a jewel. On this foundation of the story the characters are raised: and, since no story can afford characters enough for the variety of the English stage, it follows that it is to be altered and enlarged with new persons, accidents, and designs, which will almost make it new.

17. The *Hecatommithi* (1565) was not a source for *Romeo and Juliet*, though it was for *Othello* and several other Shakespearian plays.

When this is done, the forming it into acts and scenes, disposing of actions and passions into their proper places, and beautifying both with descriptions, similitudes, and propriety of language, is the principal employment of the poet; as being the largest field of fancy, which is the principal quality required in him: for so much the word ποιητής [maker, i.e. poet] implies. Judgment, indeed, is necessary in him; but 'tis fancy that gives the life-touches, and the secret graces to it; especially in serious plays, which depend not much on observation. For to write humour in comedy (which is the theft of poets from mankind), little of fancy is required; the poet observes only what is ridiculous and pleasant folly, and by judging exactly what is so, he pleases in the representation of it.

But in general, the employment of a poet is like that of a curious gunsmith or watchmaker: the iron or silver is not his own; but they are the least part of that which gives the value: the price lies wholly in the workmanship. And he who works dully on a story, without moving laughter in a comedy, or raising concernments in a serious play, is no more to be accounted a good poet than a gunsmith of the Minories [18] is to be compared with the best workman of the town.

But I have said more of this than I intended; and more, perhaps, than I needed to have done. I shall but laugh at them hereafter who accuse me with so little reason; and withal condemn their dullness who, if they could ruin that little reputation I have got, and which I value not, yet would want both wit and learning to establish their own; or to be remembered in after ages for anything but only that which makes them ridiculous in this.

"Preface," in *An Evening's Love, or The Mock Astrologer* ([London]: printed by T. N. for Henry Herringman, 1671), sigs. A4–a4v.

18. A street in London known for its armorers.

# The Author's Apology for Heroic Poetry and Heroic Licence

## Prefixed to

## *The State of Innocence: An Opera*
## (1677)

*Dryden always admired what he once referred to as "a vigorous and masculine wit," and one of the great virtues of his verse is that although he establishes and adheres to most of the neoclassical proprieties, he also keeps much of the momentum and metaphorical energy of earlier seventeenth-century poetry. "The Author's Apology" is his most unequivocal defense of this inheritance. It is written under the influence of Longinus' treatise* On the Sublime, *which he had recently read in a French translation, but his arguments are essentially the same as those which he had already used to justify rhyme in tragedy and repartee in comedy. Ostensibly his case is purely theoretical, based upon the principle of decorum: since the epic genre by definition deals with elevated and sublime subjects, "all reasonable men will conclude it necessary that sublime subjects ought to be adorned with the sublimest, and (consequently often) with the most figurative expressions." But he also resorts to a defense which is more empirical, for he argues, as he had with rhyme and repartee, that it is the consciousness of the author's very difficulties in bringing off daring figurative expressions that gives the reader the greatest pleasure. "I will presume for once to tell them," he remarks, "that the boldest strokes of poetry, when they are managed artfully, are those which most delight the reader."*

To satisfy the curiosity of those who will give themselves the trouble of reading the ensuing poem, I think myself obliged to render them a reason why I publish an opera which was never acted. In the first place, I shall not be ashamed to own that my chiefest motive was the ambition which I acknowledged in the Epistle.[1] I was desirous to lay at the feet of so beautiful and excellent a Princess a work which, I confess, was unworthy her, but which I hope she will have the goodness to forgive. I was also induced to it in my own defense; many hundred copies of it being dispersed abroad without my knowledge or consent: so that everyone gathering new faults, it became at length a libel against me; and I saw, with some disdain, more nonsense than either I, or as bad a poet, could have crammed into it at a month's warning; in which time 'twas wholly written, and not since revised. After this, I cannot, without injury to the deceased author of *Paradise Lost*, but acknowledge that this poem has received its entire foundation, part of the design, and many of the ornaments, from him. What I have borrowed will be so easily discerned from my mean productions, that I shall not need to point the reader to the places: and truly I should be sorry, for my own sake, that anyone should take the pains to compare them together; the original being undoubtedly one of the greatest, most noble, and most sublime poems which either this age or nation has produced. And though I could not refuse the partiality of my friend who is pleased to commend me in his verses,[2] I hope they will rather be esteemed the effect of his love to me than of his deliberate and sober judgment. His genius is able to make beautiful what he pleases: yet, as he has been too favorable to me, I doubt not but he will hear of his kindness from many of our contemporaries. For we are fallen into an age of illiterate, censorious, and detracting people who, thus qualified, set up for critics.

In the first place, I must take leave to tell them that they wholly mistake the nature of criticism who think its business is principally to find fault. Criticism, as it was first instituted by Aristotle, was meant a standard of judging well; the chiefest part of which is to observe those excellencies which should delight a reasonable reader. If the design, the conduct, the thoughts, and the expressions of a

1. The dedicatory epistle to the Duchess of York, which preceded "The Author's Apology."

2. Nathaniel Lee, a dramatist with whom Dryden was soon to collaborate on a play, contributed commendatory verses to *The State of Innocence*.

poem be generally such as proceed from a true genius of poetry, the critic ought to pass his judgment in favor of the author. 'Tis malicious and unmanly to snarl at the little lapses of a pen from which Virgil himself stands not exempted. Horace acknowledges that honest Homer nods sometimes: he is not equally awake in every line; but he leaves it also as a standing measure for our judgments,

> when there are numerous beauties in a poem, I will not be offended by a few blemishes which have been dropped by a careless hand or which human frailty has been unable to avert.[3]

And Longinus, who was undoubtedly, after Aristotle, the greatest critic amongst the Greeks, in his twenty-seventh chapter ΠΕΡΙ ΥΨΟΥΣ [On the Sublime],[4] has judiciously preferred the sublime genius that sometimes errs to the middling or indifferent one which makes few faults, but seldom or never rises to any excellence. He compares the first to a man of large possessions who has not leisure to consider of every slight expense, will not debase himself to the management of every trifle: particular sums are not laid out or spared to the greatest advantage in his economy, but are sometimes suffered to run to waste, while he is only careful of the main. On the other side, he likens the mediocrity of wit to one of a mean fortune, who manages his store with extreme frugality, or rather parsimony; but who, with fear of running into profuseness, never arrives to the magnificence of living. This kind of genius writes indeed correctly. A wary man he is in grammar: very nice as to solecism or barbarism, judges to a hair of little decencies, knows better than any man what is not to be written, and never hazards himself so far as to fall, but plods on deliberately and, as a grave man ought, is sure to put his staff before him; in short, he sets his heart upon it, and with wonderful care makes his business sure; that is, in plain English, neither to be blamed nor praised. I could, says my author, find out some blemishes in Homer; and am, perhaps, as naturally inclined to be disgusted at a fault as another man; but

---

3. *non, ubi plura nitent in carmine, paucis*
   *offendar maculis, quas aut incuria fudit,*
   *aut humana parum cavit natura.*
         *Ars poetica*, ll. 351–353.
4. Recently translated into French by Boileau (1674).

after all, to speak impartially, his failings are such as are only
marks of human frailty: they are little mistakes, or rather negli-
gences, which have escaped his pen in the fervor of his writing;
the sublimity of his spirit carries it with me against his carelessness;
and though Apollonius his *Argonauts*, and Theocritus his *Eidullia*,
are more free from errors, there is not any man of so false a judgment
who would choose rather to have been Apollonius or Theocritus
than Homer.

'Tis worth our consideration a little to examine how much these
hypercritics of English poetry differ from the opinion of the Greek
and Latin judges of antiquity; from the Italians and French who
have succeeded them; and, indeed, from the general taste and
approbation of all ages. Heroic poetry, which they contemn, has
ever been esteemed, and ever will be, the greatest work of human
nature: in that rank has Aristotle placed it; and Longinus is so
full of the like expressions that he abundantly confirms the other
testimony. Horace as plainly delivers his opinion, and particularly
praises Homer in these verses:

> My dear Lollius Maximus, while you declaim in Rome, I, at Praeneste,
> have reread the poet of the Trojan war; who shows more fully and with
> better effect than Chrysippus and Crantor what is noble and what is
> base, what useful and what not.[5]

And in another place, modestly excluding himself from the number
of poets, because he only writ odes and satires, he tells you a poet is
such an one,

> whose soul is more divine and whose tongue is noble in utterance.[6]

Quotations are superfluous in an established truth: otherwise I
could reckon up, amongst the moderns, all the Italian commentators
on Aristotle's book of poetry; and amongst the French, the greatest

---

5. *Trojani Belli scriptorem, Maxime Lolli,*
   *dum tu declamas Romae, Praeneste relegi:*
   *qui quid sit pulchrum, quid turpe, quid utile, quid non,*
   *planius ac melius Chrysippo et Crantore dicit.*
   > *Epistles,* I, ii. 1–4.

6.      *cui mens divinior, atque os*
   *magna sonatorium.*
   > *Satires,* I. iv. 43–44.

of this age, Boileau and Rapin; the latter of which is alone sufficient, were all other critics lost, to teach anew the rules of writing. Any man who will seriously consider the nature of an epic poem, how it agrees with that of poetry in general, which is to instruct and to delight; what actions it describes, and what persons they are chiefly whom it informs, will find it a work which indeed is full of difficulty in the attempt, but admirable when 'tis well performed. I write not this with the least intention to undervalue the other parts of poetry: for comedy is both excellently instructive, and extremely pleasant: satire lashes vice into reformation, and humour represents folly so as to render it ridiculous. Many of our present writers are eminent in both these kinds; and particularly the author of the *Plain Dealer*,[7] whom I am proud to call my friend, has obliged all honest and virtuous men by one of the most bold, most general, and most useful satires which has ever been presented on the English theater. I do not dispute the preference of tragedy; let every man enjoy his taste: but 'tis unjust that they who have not the least notion of heroic writing should therefore condemn the pleasure which others receive from it, because they cannot comprehend it. Let them please their appetites in eating what they like; but let them not force this dish on all the table. They who would combat general authority with particular opinion must first establish themselves a reputation of understanding better than other men. Are all the flights of heroic poetry to be concluded bombast, unnatural, and mere madness, because they are not affected with their excellencies? 'Tis just as reasonable as to conclude there is no day because a blind man cannot distinguish of light and colors. Ought they not rather, in modesty, to doubt of their own judgments, when they think this or that expression in Homer, Virgil, Tasso, or Milton's *Paradise* to be too far strained, than positively to conclude that 'tis all fustian, and mere nonsense? 'Tis true, there are limits to be set betwixt the boldness and rashness of a poet; but he must understand those limits who pretends to judge as well as he who undertakes to write: and he who has no liking to the whole ought, in reason, to be excluded from censuring of the parts. He must be a lawyer before he mounts the tribunal; and the judicature of one court, too, does not

7. William Wycherley, author also of *The Country Wife*.

qualify a man to preside in another. He may be an excellent pleader in the Chancery, who is not fit to rule the Common Pleas. But I will presume for once to tell them that the boldest strokes of poetry, when they are managed artfully, are those which most delight the reader.

Virgil and Horace, the severest writers of the severest age, have made frequent use of the hardest metaphors, and of the strongest hyperboles: and in this case the best authority is the best argument. For generally to have pleased, and through all ages, must bear the force of universal tradition. And if you would appeal from thence to right reason, you will gain no more by it in effect than, first, to set up your reason against those authors; and, secondly, against all those who have admired them. You must prove why that ought not to have pleased, which has pleased the most learned and the most judicious; and to be thought knowing, you must first put the fool upon all mankind. If you can enter more deeply than they have done into the causes and resorts of that which moves pleasure in a reader, the field is open, you may be heard: but those springs of human nature are not so easily discovered by every superficial judge. It requires philosophy as well as poetry to sound the depth of all the passions; what they are in themselves, and how they are to be provoked; and in this science the best poets have excelled. Aristotle raised the fabric of his *Poetry* from observation of those things in which Euripides, Sophocles, and Aeschylus pleased: he considered how they raised the passions, and thence has drawn rules for our imitation. From hence have sprung the tropes and figures for which they wanted a name who first practiced them, and succeeded in them. Thus I grant you that the knowledge of nature was the original rule; and that all poets ought to study her, as well as Aristotle and Horace, her interpreters. But then this also undeniably follows, that those things which delight all ages must have been an imitation of nature; which is all I contend. Therefore is rhetoric made an art; therefore the names of so many tropes and figures were invented: because it was observed they had such and such effect upon the audience. Therefore catachreses and hyperboles have found their place amongst them; not that they were to be avoided, but to be used judiciously, and placed in poetry as heightenings and shadows are in painting, to make the figure bolder, and cause it to stand off to sight.

> Nets meditate no snare for stags,[8]

says Virgil in his *Eclogues*: and speaking of Leander in his *Georgics*,

> above him heaven's great archway thunders, and the waves, dashing upon the cliffs, echo the cry.[9]

In both of these, you see he fears not to give voice and thought to things inanimate.

Will you arraign your master Horace for his hardness of expression when he describes the death of Cleopatra, and says she did "handle fierce snakes, to imbibe black poison into her body,"[10] because the body in that action performs what is proper to the mouth?

As for hyperboles, I will neither quote Lucan, nor Statius, men of an unbounded imagination, but who often wanted the poise of judgment. The divine Virgil was not liable to that exception; and yet he describes Polyphemus thus:

> he strides through the sea; nor has the wave yet moistened his mighty sides.[11]

In imitation of this place, our admirable Cowley thus paints Goliah:

> The valley, now, this monster seem'd to fill;
> And we, methought, look'd up to him from our hill,[12]

8.     *nec retia cervis*
   *ulla dolum meditantur.*
      *Eclogues*, V. 60–61.
9. *caeca nocte natat serus freta, quem super ingens*
   *porta tonat coeli, et scopulis inlisa reclamant*
   *aequora.*
                              *Georgics.* 260–262.
10. "*asperos tractare serpentes, ut atrum corpore combiberet venenum*" (*Odes*, I. xxxvii 26–28).
11.     *graditurque per aequor*
   *jam medium; necdum fluctus latera ardua tingit.*
                  *Aeneid*, III. 664–665.
12. *Davideis* (1656), III. 385–386.

where the two words *seemed* and *methought* have mollified the figure, and yet if they had not been there, the fright of the Israelites might have excused their belief of the giant's stature.

In the 8th of the Æneids, Virgil paints the swiftness of Camilla thus:

> Outstripped the winds in speed upon the plain,
> Flew o'er the fields, nor hurt the bearded grain:
> She swept the seas, and as she skimmed along,
> Her flying feet unbathed on billows hung.[13]

You are not obliged, as in history, to a literal belief of what the poet says; but you are pleased with the image, without being cozened by the fiction.

Yet even in history, Longinus quotes Herodotus on this occasion of hyperboles. The Lacedemonians, says he, at the straits of Thermopylae, defended themselves to the last extremity; and when their arms failed them, fought it out with their nails and teeth; till at length (the Persians shooting continually upon them) they lay buried under the arrows of their enemies. It is not reasonable (continues the critic) to believe that men could defend themselves with their nails and teeth from an armed multitude; nor that they lay buried under a pile of darts and arrows; and yet there wants not probability for the figure: because the hyperbole seems not to have been made for the sake of the description, but rather to have been produced from the occasion.

'Tis true, the boldness of the figures are to be hidden sometimes by the address of the poet, that they may work their effect upon the mind without discovering the art which caused it. And therefore they are principally to be used in passion; when we speak more warmly, and with more precipitation, than at other times: for then, "if you wish to make me weep, you must first weep yourself";[14]

---

13. *Illa vel intactae segetis per summa volaret*
    *gramina, nec teneras cursu laesisset aristas;*
    *vel mare per medium, fluctu suspensa tumenti,*
    *ferret iter, celeres nec tingeret aequore plantas.*
                        *Aeneid*, VII. 808–811.
The translation is from Dryden's version of the *Aeneid*.
14. "*si vis me flere, dolendum est primum ipsi tibi*" (Horace, *Ars poetica*, ll. 102–103).

the poet must put on the passion he endeavors to represent: a man in such an occasion is not cool enough, either to reason rightly, or to talk calmly. Aggravations are then in their proper places; interrogations, exclamations, hyperbata, or a disordered connection of discourse, are graceful there because they are natural. The sum of all depends on what before I hinted, that this boldness of expression is not to be blamed if it be managed by the coolness and discretion which is necessary to a poet.

Yet before I leave this subject, I cannot but take notice how disingenuous our adversaries appear: all that is dull, insipid, languishing, and without sinews in a poem, they call an imitation of nature: they only offend our most equitable judges, who think beyond them; and lively images and elocution are never to be forgiven.

What fustian, as they call it, have I heard these gentlemen find out in Mr. Cowley's *Odes*! I acknowledge myself unworthy to defend so excellent an author, neither have I room to do it here; only in general I will say that nothing can appear more beautiful to me than the strength of those images which they condemn.

Imaging is, in itself, the very height and life of poetry. It is, as Longinus describes it, a discourse, which by a kind of enthusiasm, or extraordinary emotion of the soul, makes it seem to us that we behold those things which the poet paints, so as to be pleased with them, and to admire them.

If poetry be imitation, that part of it must needs be best which describes most lively our actions and passions, our virtues and our vices, our follies and our humours: for neither is comedy without its part of imaging; and they who do it best are certainly the most excellent in their kind. This is too plainly proved to be denied. But how are poetical fictions, how are hippocentaurs and chimeras, or how are angels and immaterial substances to be imaged; which, some of them, are things quite out of nature; others, such whereof we can have no notion? This is the last refuge of our adversaries; and more than any of them have yet had the wit to object against us. The answer is easy to the first part of it. The fiction of some beings which are not in nature (second notions, as the logicians call them) has been founded on the conjunction of two natures which have a real separate being. So hippocentaurs were imagined by joining the natures of a man and horse together; as Lucretius tell us, who has used this word of *image* oftener than any of the poets:

> the image of a centaur is certainly not drawn from life, since no such living creature ever existed: but where images of horse and man meet by chance, they may readily combine.[15]

The same reason may also be alleged for chimeras and the rest. And poets may be allowed the like liberty for describing things which really exist not, if they are founded on popular belief. Of this nature are fairies, pigmies, and the extraordinary effects of magic; for 'tis still an imitation, though of other men's fancies: and thus are Shakespeare's *Tempest*, his *Midsummer Night's Dream*, and Ben Jonson's *Masque of Witches*[16] to be defended. For immaterial substances, we are authorized by Scripture in their description: and herein the text accommodates itself to vulgar apprehension, in giving angels the likeness of beautiful young men. Thus, after the pagan divinity, has Homer drawn his gods with human faces: and thus we have notions of things above us, by describing them like other beings more within our knowledge.

I wish I could produce any one example of excellent imaging in all this poem: perhaps I cannot; but that which comes nearest it is in these four lines, which have been sufficiently canvassed by my well-natured censors:

> Seraph and cherub, careless of their charge,
> And wanton, in full ease now live at large:
> Unguarded leave the passes of the sky,
> And all dissolved in hallelujahs lie.[17]

I have heard (says one of them) of anchovies dissolved in sauce; but never of an angel in hallelujahs. A mighty witticism (if you will pardon a new word!) but there is some difference between a laugher

15.  *nam certe ex vivo centauri non fit imago,*
     *nulla fuit quoniam talis natura animai:*
     *verum ubi equi atque hominis casu, convenit imago,*
     *haerescit facile extemplo, etc.*
                         *De rerum natura,* iv. 739–742.

16.  *The Masque of Queens* (1616) is the correct title. It was first performed in 1609.

17.  *The State of Innocence,* I, i.

and a critic. He might have burlesqued Virgil too, from whom I
took the image: "they invade the city, buried in sleep and wine."[18]
A city's being buried is just as proper on occasion as an angel's
being dissolved in ease and songs of triumph. Mr. Cowley lies as
open too in many places:

Where their vast courts the mother waters keep, etc.[19]

For if the mass of waters be the mothers, then their daughters, the
little streams, are bound, in all good manners, to make courtesy
to them, and ask them blessing. How easy 'tis to turn into ridicule
the best descriptions, when once a man is in the humour of laughing
till he wheezes at his own dull jest! But an image which is strongly
and beautifully set before the eyes of the reader will still be poetry
when the merry fit is over: and last when the other is forgotten.

I promised to say somewhat of poetic license, but have in part
anticipated my discourse already. Poetic license I take to be the
liberty, which poets have assumed to themselves in all ages, of
speaking things in verse which are beyond the severity of prose.
'Tis that particular character which distinguishes and sets the
bounds betwixt *oratio soluta*[20] [prose] and poetry. This, as to what
regards the thought or imagination of a poet, consists in fiction:
but then those thoughts must be expressed; and here arise two other
branches of it: for if this license be included in a single word, it
admits of tropes; if in a sentence or proposition, of figures; both
which are of a much larger extent, and more forcibly to be used in
verse than prose. This is that birthright which is derived to us from
our great forefathers, even from Homer down to Ben. And they
who would deny it to us have, in plain terms, the fox's quarrel to the
grapes: they cannot reach it.

How far these liberties are to be extended, I will not presume
to determine here, since Horace does not. But it is certain that
they are to be varied, according to the language and age in which
an author writes. That which would be allowed to a Grecian poet,
Martial tells you, would not be suffered in a Roman. And 'tis

18. *"invadunt urbem, somno vinoque sepultam"* (*Aeneid*, II. 265).
19. *Davideis*, I. 79.
20. Cicero's term for prose.

evident that the English does more nearly follow the strictness of the latter than the freedoms of the former. Connection of epithets, or the conjunction of two words in one, are frequent and elegant in the Greek, which yet Sir Philip Sidney, and the translator of Du Bartas, have unluckily attempted in the English; though this, I confess, is not so proper an instance of poetic license, as it is of variety of idiom in languages.

Horace a little explains himself on this subject of *licentia poetica*, in these verses:

> painters and poets have always had an equal right to license, but not to mate the savage with the tame, or to pair serpents with birds and lambs with tigers.[21]

He would have a poem of a piece; not to begin with one thing and end with another: he restrains it so far that thoughts of an unlike nature ought not to be joined together. That were indeed to make a chaos. He taxed not Homer, nor the divine Virgil, for interesting their gods in the wars of Troy and Italy; neither, had he now lived, would he have taxed Milton, as our false critics have presumed to do, for his choice of a supernatural argument: but he would have blamed my author, who was a Christian, had he introduced into his poem heathen deities, as Tasso is condemned by Rapin on the like occasion; and as Camoens, the author of the *Lusiads*, ought to be censured by all his readers when he brings in Bacchus and Christ into the same adventure of his fable.[22]

From that which has been said, it may be collected that the definition of wit (which has been so often attempted, and ever unsuccessfully by many poets) is only this: that it is a propriety of thoughts and words; or, in other terms, thoughts and words elegantly adapted to the subject. If our critics will join issue on this definition, that we may *convenire in aliquo tertio* [agree upon some

---

21.      *pictoribus atque poetis*
    *quidlibet audendi semper fuit aequa potestas:*
    *sed non, ut placidis coeant immitia, non ut*
    *serpentes avibus geminentur, tigribus haedi.*
        *Ars poetica*, ll. 9–10, 12–13.

22. Rapin did not condemn Tasso on this account, although he did censure Camoëns.

intermediate position]; if they will take it as a granted principle, 'twill be easy to put an end to this dispute. No man will disagree from another's judgment concerning the dignity of style in heroic poetry; but all reasonable men will conclude it necessary that sublime subjects ought to be adorned with the sublimest, and (consequently often) with the most figurative expressions. In the meantime, I will not run into their fault of imposing my opinions on other men, any more than I would my writings on their taste: I have only laid down, and that superficially enough, my present thoughts; and shall be glad to be taught better by those who pretend to reform our poetry.

"The Authors Apology for Heroique Poetry; and Poetique Licence," in *The State of Innocence, and Fall of Man: An Opera* (London: printed by T. N. for Henry Herringman, 1677), sigs. b1–c2v.

# Heads of an Answer to Rymer
## (1677)

*The "Heads of an Answer" consists of notes which Dryden made in his copy, now lost, of Thomas Rymer's* Tragedies of the Last Age *(1677). Two authoritative texts of the notes have survived: the publisher Tonson's, which is the basis of this edition, and Samuel Johnson's. Johnson's order of the notes is: paragraphs 34, 51–53, 35–38, 1–6, 28–33, 39–50, 7–28. (See "A Note on the Texts," above, p. xvii.)*

*In the* Tragedies of the Last Age *Rymer attacked the English dramatic tradition by applying to it the precepts and examples of the classical theater. Dryden's answer in these notes is simple and penetrating. He points out that, notwithstanding all of Rymer's strictures, English plays do move readers and spectators, they "please the English," and "the poet's business is certainly to please his audience." He adds that "'tis not enough that Aristotle has said so, for Aristotle drew his models of tragedy from Sophocles and Euripides; and if he had seen ours, might have changed his mind." The trenchancy of this argument, as of most of the "Heads of an Answer," lies in its clear appreciation of the distinction between practice and theory, between the actual experience of literature and mere hypotheses about it.*

1] He who undertakes to answer this exellent critique of Mr. Rymer, in behalf of our English poets against the Greek, ought to do it in this manner.

2] Either by yielding to him the greatest part of what he contends for, which consists in this, that the μῦθος, i.e. the design and conduct of it, is more conducing in the Greeks to those ends of tragedy which Aristotle and he propose, namely to cause terror and pity; yet the granting this does not set the Greeks above the English poets.

3] But the answerer ought to prove two things: first, that the fable is not the greatest masterpiece of a tragedy, tho' it be the foundation of it.

4] Secondly, that other ends as suitable to the nature of tragedy may be found in the English, which were not in the Greek.

5] Aristotle places the fable first; not *quoad dignitatem, sed quoad fundamentum* [because of its dignity, but because of its priority]; for a fable, never so movingly contrived to those ends of his, pity and terror, will operate nothing on our affections, except the characters, manners, thoughts, and words are suitable.

6] So that it remains for Mr. Rymer to prove that in all those, or the greatest part of them, we are inferior to Sophocles and Euripides; and this he has offered at in some measure, but, I think, a little partially to the Ancients.

7] To make a true judgment in this competition between the Greek poets and the English in tragedy, consider

    I. How Aristotle has defined a tragedy.
   II. What he assigns the end of it to be.
 III. What he thinks the beauties of it.
 IV. The means to attain the end proposed.

Compare the Greek and English tragic poets justly and without partiality, according to those rules.

8] Then, secondly, consider whether Aristotle has made a just definition of tragedy, of its parts, of its end, of its beauties; and whether he, having not seen any others but those of Sophocles, Euripides, etc., had or truly could determine what all the excellencies of tragedy are, and wherein they consist.

9] Next show in what ancient tragedy was deficient: for example, in the narrowness of its plots, and fewness of persons, and try whether that be not a fault in the Greek poets; and whether their excellency was so great when the variety was visibly so little; or whether what they did was not very easy to do.

10] Then make a judgment on what the English have added to their beauties: as, for example, not only more plot, but also new passions;

as namely, that of love, scarce touched on by the Ancients, except in this one example of Phaedra, cited by Mr. Rymer; and in that how short they were of Fletcher.

11] Prove also that love, being an heroic passion, is fit for tragedy, which cannot be denied, because of the example alleged of Phaedra; and how far Shakespeare has outdone them in friendship, etc.

12] To return to the beginning of this enquiry: consider if pity and terror be enough for tragedy to move; and I believe, upon a true definition of tragedy, it will be found that its work extends farther, and that it is to reform manners by delightful representation of human life in great persons, by way of dialogue. If this be true, then not only pity and terror are to be moved as the only means to bring us to virtue, but generally love to virtue and hatred to vice; by showing the rewards of one, and punishments of the other; at least by rendering virtue always amiable, though it be shown unfortunate; and vice detestable, tho' it be shown triumphant.

13] If then the encouragement of virtue and discouragement of vice be the proper ends of poetry in tragedy: pity and terror, tho' good means, are not the only. For all the passions in their turns are to be set in a ferment: as joy, anger, love, fear are to be used as the poet's commonplaces; and a general concernment for the principal actors is to be raised by making them appear such in their characters, their words, and actions, as will interest the audience in their fortunes.

14] And if after all, in a large sense, pity comprehends this concernment for the good, and terror includes detestation for the bad, then let us consider whether the English have not answered this end of tragedy as well as the Ancients, or perhaps better.

15] And here Mr. Rymer's objections against these plays are to be impartially weighed, that we may see whether they are of weight enough to turn the balance against our countrymen.

16] 'Tis evident those plays which he arraigns[1] have moved both those passions in a high degree upon the stage.

---

1. *Rollo, or The Bloody Brother; A King and No King;* and *The Maid's Tragedy,* all by Beaumont and Fletcher, and all extremely popular in revivals on the Restoration stage.

17] To give the glory of this away from the poet, and to place it upon the actors, seems unjust.[2]

18] One reason is, because whatever actors they have found, the event has been the same, that is, the same passions have been always moved; which shows that there is something of force and merit in the plays themselves, conducing to the design of raising these two passions: and suppose them ever to have been excellently acted, yet action only adds grace, vigor, and more life upon the stage; but cannot give it wholly where it is not first. But secondly, I dare appeal to those who have never seen them acted, if they have not found those two passions moved within them; and if the general voice will carry it, Mr. Rymer's prejudice will take off his single testimony.

19] This, being matter of fact, is reasonably to be established by this appeal; as if one man says 'tis night, when the rest of the world conclude it to be day, there needs no further argument against him that it is so.

20] If he urge that the general taste is depraved, his arguments to prove this can at best but evince that our poets took not the best way to raise those passions; but experience proves against him that those means which they have used have been successful and have produced them.

21] And one reason of that success is, in my opinion, this, that Shakespeare and Fletcher have written to the genius of the age and nation in which they lived; for tho' nature, as he objects, is the same in all places, and reason too the same, yet the climate, the age, the dispositions of the people to whom a poet writes may be so different that what pleased the Greeks would not satisfy an English audience.

22] And if they proceeded upon a foundation of truer reason to please the Athenians than Shakespeare and Fletcher to please the English, it only shows that the Athenians were a more judicious people; but the poet's business is certainly to please the audience.

23] Whether our English audience have been pleased hitherto with acorns, as he calls it, or with bread, is the next question; that is,

---

2. Rymer had claimed that it was the actors' abilities rather than intrinsic merit which accounted for the success of the plays on stage.

whether the means which Shakespeare and Fletcher have used in their plays to raise those passions before named, be better applied to the ends by the Greek poets than by them; and perhaps we shall not grant him this wholly. Let it be yielded that a writer is not to run down with the stream, or to please the people by their own usual methods, but rather to reform their judgments: it still remains to prove that our theater needs this total reformation.

24] The faults which he has found in their designs are rather wittily aggravated in many places than reasonably urged; and as much may be returned on the Greeks by one who were as witty as himself.

25] Secondly, they destroy not, if they are granted, the foundation of the fabric, only take away from the beauty of the symmetry: for example, the faults in the character of the King and No King are not, as he makes them, such as render him detestable, but only imperfections which accompany human nature, and for the most part excused by the violence of his love; so that they destroy not our pity or concernment for him. This answer may be applied to most of his objections of that kind.

26] And Rollo committing many murders, when he is answerable but for one, is too severely arraigned by him; for it adds to our horror and detestation of the criminal; and poetic justice is not neglected neither, for we stab him in our minds for every offence which he commits; and the point which the poet is to gain on the audience is not so much in the death of an offender, as the raising an horror of his crimes.

27] That the criminal should neither be wholly guilty, nor wholly innocent, but so participating of both as to move both pity and terror, is certainly a good rule, but not perpetually to be observed: for that were to make all tragedies too much alike; which objection he foresaw, but has not fully answered.

28] To conclude, therefore: if the plays of the Ancients are more correctly plotted, ours are more beautifully written; and if we can raise passions as high on worse foundations, it shows our genius in tragedy is greater, for in all other parts of it the English have manifestly excelled them.

29] For the fable itself, 'tis in the English more adorned with episodes, and larger than in the Greek poets; consequently more diverting. For, if the action be but one, and that plain, without any counter-turn of design or episode, *i.e.* under-plot, how can it be so pleasing as the English, which have both under-plot and a turned design, which keeps the audience in expectation of the catastrophe? whereas in the Greek poets we see through the whole design at first.

30] For the characters, they are neither so many nor so various in Sophocles and Euripides as in Shakespeare and Fletcher; only they are more adapted to those ends of tragedy which Aristotle commends to us: pity and terror.

31] The manners flow from the characters, and consequently must partake of their advantages and disadvantages.

32] The thoughts and words, which are the fourth and fifth beauties of tragedy, are certainly more noble and more poetical in the English than in the Greek, which must be proved by comparing them somewhat more equitably than Mr. Rymer has done.

33] After all, we need not yield that the English way is less conducing to move pity and terror, because they often show virtue oppressed and vice punished: where they do not both, or either, they are not to be defended.

34] That we may the less wonder why pity and terror are not now the only springs on which our tragedies move, and that Shakespeare may be more excused, Rapin confesses that the French tragedies now all run upon the *tendre* [tender]; and gives the reason, because love is the passion which most predominates in our souls, and that therefore the passions represented become insipid, unless they are conformable to the thoughts of the audience. But it is to be concluded that this passion works not now among the French so strongly as the other two did amongst the Ancients. Amongst us, who have a stronger genius for writing, the operations from the writing are much stronger; for the raising of Shakespeare's passions are more from the excellency of the words and thoughts than the justness of the occasion; and if he has been able to pick single occasions, he has never founded the whole reasonably; yet by the genius of poetry, in writing he has succeeded.

35] The parts of a poem, tragic or heroic, are:

I. The fable itself.
II. The order or manner of its contrivance in relation of the parts to the whole.
III. The manners or decency of the characters in speaking or acting what is proper for them, and proper to be shown by the poet.
IV. The thoughts which express the manners.
V. The words which express those thoughts.

36] In the last of these Homer excels Virgil, Virgil all other ancient poets, and Shakespeare all modern poets.

37] For the second of these, the order: the meaning is that a fable ought to have a beginning, middle, and an end, all just and natural, so that that part which is the middle could not naturally be the beginning or end, and so of the rest: all are depending on one another, like the links of a curious chain.

38] If terror and pity are only to be raised, certainly this author follows Aristotle's rules, and Sophocles's and Euripides's example; but joy may be raised too, and that doubly, either by seeing a wicked man punished, or a good man at last fortunate; or perhaps indignation, to see wickedness prosperous and goodness depressed: both these may be profitable to the end of tragedy, reformation of manners; but the last improperly, only as it begets pity in the audience: tho' Aristotle, I confess, places tragedies of this kind in the second form.

39] And, if we should grant that the Greeks performed this better, perhaps it may admit a dispute whether pity and terror are either the prime, or at least the only ends of tragedy.

40] 'Tis not enough that Aristotle has said so, for Aristotle drew his models of tragedy from Sophocles and Euripides; and if he had seen ours, might have changed his mind.

41] And chiefly we have to say (what I hinted on pity and terror in the last paragraph save one)[3] that the punishment of vice and reward of virtue are the most adequate ends of tragedy, because most conducing to good example of life. Now pity is not so easily raised for a criminal (and the ancient tragedy always represented its

3. Apparently in paragraph 38, above.

chief person such) as it is for an innocent man, and the suffering of innocence and punishment of the offender is of the nature of English tragedy: contrarily, in the Greek, innocence is unhappy often, and the offender escapes.

42] Then, we are not touched with the sufferings of any sort of men so much as of lovers; and this was almost unknown to the Ancients; so that they neither administered poetical justice (of which Mr. Rymer boasts) so well as we; neither knew they the best commonplace of pity, which is love.

43] He therefore unjustly blames us for not building on what the Ancients left us, for it seems, upon consideration of the premises, that we have wholly finished what they began.

44] My judgment on this piece is this, that it is extremely learned; but that the author of it is better read in the Greek than in the English poets; that all writers ought to study this critique as the best account I have ever seen of the Ancients; that the model of tragedy he has here given is excellent and extreme correct; but that it is not the only model of all tragedy, because it is too much circumscribed in plot, characters, etc.; and lastly, that we may be taught here justly to admire and imitate the Ancients, without giving them the preference, with this author, in prejudice to our own country.

45] Want of method in this excellent treatise makes the thoughts of the author sometimes obscure.

46] His meaning, that pity and terror are to be moved, is that they are to be moved as the means conducing to the ends of tragedy, which are pleasure and instruction.

47] And these two ends may be thus distinguished. The chief end of the poet is to please; for his immediate reputation depends on it.

48] The great end of the poem is to instruct, which is performed by making pleasure the vehicle of that instruction; for poetry is an art, and all arts are made to profit.

49] The pity which the poet is to labor for is for the criminal, not for those, or him, whom he has murdered, or who have been the occasion of the tragedy. The terror is likewise in the punishment of the same criminal who, if he be represented too great an offender, will not be pitied; if altogether innocent, his punishment will be unjust.

50] Another obscurity is where he says Sophocles perfected tragedy by introducing the third actor; that is, he meant three kinds of action, one company singing or speaking, another playing on the music, a third dancing.

51] Rapin attributes more to the *dictio*, that is, to the words and discourses of a tragedy, than Aristotle has done, who places them in the last rank of beauties; perhaps only last in order, because they are the last product of the design, of the disposition or connection of its parts; of the characters, of the manners of those characters, and of the thoughts proceeding from those manners.

52] Rapin's words are remarkable: "'Tis not the admirable intrigue, the surprising events, and extraordinary incidents that make the beauty of a tragedy; 'tis the discourses when they are natural and passionate." [4]

53] So are Shakespeare's.

"Heads of an Answer to Rymer," printed in the Preface to *The Works of Mr. Francis Beaumont, and Mr. John Fletcher* (London: printed for Jacob Tonson, 1711), I, xii–xxvi.

4. *Réflexions sur la poétique d'Aristote* (1674), I. xxvi.

# Preface to
## *Troilus and Cressida*

# Containing the Grounds of Criticism
# in Tragedy
# (1679)

*The stimulus of this essay is clearly Rymer's* Tragedies of the Last Age *(1677), but whereas in the "Heads of an Answer" Dryden questioned Rymer's fundamental assumptions, here he does not. As a result, the essay is not penetrating, and it represents Dryden's least successful attempt to find meaningful public expression for his own experience and instincts. It is also significant as a reflection of the growing tendency in the drama and criticism of the time to place primary emphasis upon tragedy's capacity to arouse emotions, especially the emotion of pity, which Dryden calls the "most god-like of moral virtues."*

The poet Æschylus was held in the same veneration by the Athenians of after ages as Shakespeare is by us; and Longinus has judged, in favor of him, that he had a noble boldness of expression, and that his imaginations were lofty and heroic; but, on the other side, Quintilian affirms that he was daring to extravagance. 'Tis certain that he affected pompous words, and that his sense too often was obscured by figures. Notwithstanding these imperfections, the value of his writings after his decease was such that his countrymen ordained an equal reward to those poets who could alter his plays to be acted on the theater, with those whose productions were wholly new, and of their own. The case is not the same in England; though the difficulties of altering are greater, and our reverence for Shakespeare much more just, than that of the Grecians for Æschylus. In the age of that poet, the Greek tongue was arrived to its full perfection; they had then amongst them an exact standard of writing and of speaking. The English language is not capable of such a certainty; and we are at present so far from it that we are wanting in the very foundation of it, a perfect grammar. Yet it must be allowed to the present age that the tongue in general is so much refined since Shakespeare's time that many of his words, and more of his phrases, are scarce intelligible. And of those which we understand, some are ungrammatical, others coarse; and his whole style is so pestered with figurative expressions, that it is as affected as it is obscure. 'Tis true, that in his later plays he had worn off somewhat of the rust; but the tragedy which I have undertaken to correct was, in all probability, one of his first endeavors on the stage.[1]

The original story was written by one Lollius, a Lombard, in Latin verse, and translated by Chaucer into English; intended, I suppose, a satire on the inconstancy of women: I find nothing of it among the Ancients; not so much as the name Cressida once mentioned. Shakespeare (as I hinted), in the apprenticeship of his writing, modeled it into that play which is now called by the name of *Troilus and Cressida*; but so lamely is it left to us, that it is not divided into acts; which fault I ascribe to the actors who printed it after Shakespeare's death; and that too so carelessly, that a more uncorrect copy I never saw. For the play itself, the author seems to have begun it with some fire; the characters of Pandarus and Thersites are promising enough; but as if he grew weary of his task, after an entrance or two, he lets 'em fall: and the later part of the tragedy is nothing but a confusion of drums and trumpets, excursions and alarms. The chief persons, who give name to the tragedy, are left alive; Cressida is false, and is not punished. Yet after all, because the play was Shakespeare's, and that there appeared in some places of it the admirable genius of the author, I undertook

---

1. Actually, *Troilus and Cressida*, which was probably written around 1602, came at the mid-point of Shakespeare's career.

to remove that heap of rubbish under which many excellent thoughts lay wholly buried. Accordingly, I new modeled the plot; threw out many unnecessary persons; improved those characters which were begun and left unfinished: as Hector, Troilus, Pandarus, and Thersites; and added that of Andromache. After this I made, with no small trouble, an order and connection of all the scenes; removing them from the places where they were inartificially set; and though it was impossible to keep 'em all unbroken, because the scene must be sometimes in the city and sometimes in the camp, yet I have so ordered them that there is a coherence of 'em with one another, and a dependence on the main design: no leaping from Troy to the Grecian tents, and thence back again in the same act; but a due proportion of time allowed for every motion. I need not say that I have refined his language, which before was obsolete; but I am willing to acknowledge that as I have often drawn his English nearer to our times, so I have sometimes conformed my own to his; and consequently, the language is not altogether so pure as it is significant. The scenes of Pandarus and Cressida, of Troilus and Pandarus, of Andromache with Hector and the Trojans, in the second act, are wholly new; together with that of Nestor and Ulysses with Thersites, and that of Thersites with Ajax and Achilles. I will not weary my reader with the scenes which are added of Pandarus and the lovers, in the third; and those of Thersites, which are wholly altered; but I cannot omit the last scene in it, which is almost half the act, betwixt Troilus and Hector. The occasion of raising it was hinted to me by Mr. Betterton: the contrivance and working of it was my own. They who think to do me an injury by saying that it is an imitation of the scene betwixt Brutus and Cassius, do me an honor by supposing I could imitate the incomparable Shakespeare; but let me add that if Shakespeare's scene, or that faulty copy of it in *Amintor and Melantius*, had never been, yet Euripides had furnished me with an excellent example in his *Iphigenia*, between Agamemnon and Menelaus; and from thence, indeed, the last turn of it is borrowed.[2] The occasion which Shakespeare,

2. The comparison of the quarrels between Amintor and Melantius in Beaumont and Fletcher's *Maid's Tragedy* and Agamemnon and Menelaus in Euripides's *Iphigenia in Aulis* had already been made by Rymer in his *Tragedies of the Last Age* (1678), as Dryden acknowledges in the following paragraph.

Euripides, and Fletcher have all taken is the same; grounded upon friendship: and the quarrel of two virtuous men, raised by natural degrees to the extremity of passion, is conducted in all three to the declination of the same passion, and concludes with a warm renewing of their friendship. But the particular groundwork which Shakespeare has taken is incomparably the best; because he has not only chosen two of the greatest heroes of their age, but has likewise interested the liberty of Rome, and their own honors who were the redeemers of it, in this debate. And if he has made Brutus, who was naturally a patient man, to fly into excess at first, let it be remembered in his defense that, just before, he has received the news of Portia's death; whom the poet, on purpose neglecting a little chronology, supposes to have died before Brutus, only to give him an occasion of being more easily exasperated. Add to this that the injury he had received from Cassius had long been brooding in his mind; and that a melancholy man, upon consideration of an affront, especially from a friend, would be more eager in his passion than he who had given it, though naturally more choleric.

Euripides, whom I have followed, has raised the quarrel betwixt two brothers who were friends. The foundation of the scene was this: the Grecians were windbound at the port of Aulis, and the oracle had said that they could not sail, unless Agamemnon delivered up his daughter to be sacrificed: he refuses; his brother Menelaus urges the public safety; the father defends himself by arguments of natural affection, and hereupon they quarrel. Agamemnon is at last convinced, and promises to deliver up Iphigenia, but so passionately laments his loss that Menelaus is grieved to have been the occasion of it and, by a return of kindness, offers to intercede for him with the Grecians, that his daughter might not be sacrificed. But my friend Mr. Rymer has so largely, and with so much judgment, described this scene, in comparing it with that of Melantius and Amintor, that it is superfluous to say more of it; I only named the heads of it, that any reasonable man might judge it was from thence I modeled my scene betwixt Troilus and Hector. I will conclude my reflections on it with a passage of Longinus, concerning Plato's imitation of Homer: "We ought not to regard a good imitation as a theft, but as a beautiful idea of him who undertakes to imitate, by forming himself on the invention and the work of another man; for he enters into the lists like a new wrestler, to dispute the prize with the former champion. This sort of emulation, says Hesiod, is honorable, 'this strife is wholesome to man,'[3] when we combat for victory with a hero, and are not without glory even in our overthrow. Those great men whom we propose to ourselves as patterns of our imitation serve us as a torch, which is lifted up before us to enlighten our passage; and often elevate our thoughts as high as the conception we have of our author's genius."[4]

I have been so tedious in three acts that I shall contract myself in the two last. The beginning scenes of the fourth act are either added or changed wholly by me; the middle of it is Shakespeare altered, and mingled with my own; three or four of the last scenes are altogether new. And the whole fifth act, both the plot and the writing, are my own additions.

But having written so much for imitation of what is excellent, in that part of the preface which related only to myself, methinks it would neither be unprofitable nor unpleasant to inquire how far we ought to imitate our own poets, Shakespeare and Fletcher, in their tragedies: and this will occasion another inquiry, how those two writers differ between themselves. But since neither of these questions can be solved unless some measures be first taken by which we may be enabled to judge truly of their writings, I shall endeavor, as briefly as I can, to discover the grounds and reason of all criticism, applying them in this place only to tragedy. Aristotle with his interpreters, and Horace, and Longinus, are the authors to whom I owe my lights; and what part soever of my own plans, or of this, which no mending could make regular, shall fall under the condemnation of such judges, it would be impudence in me to defend. I think it no shame to retract my errors, and am well pleased to suffer in the cause, if the art may be improved at my expense: I therefore proceed to

## THE GROUNDS OF CRITICISM IN TRAGEDY.

Tragedy is thus defined by Aristotle (omitting what I thought unnecessary in his definition). 'Tis an imitation of one entire, great,

3. "ἀγαθὴ δ' ἔρις ἐστὶ βροτοῖσιν" (*Works and Days*, l. 24).
4. *On the Sublime*, xiii. 4.

and probable action; not told, but represented; which, by moving in us fear and pity, is conducive to the purging of those two passions in our minds. More largely thus, tragedy describes or paints an action, which action must have all the proprieties above named. First, it must be one or single, that is, it must not be a history of one man's life; suppose of Alexander the Great, or Julius Caesar, but one single action of theirs. This condemns all Shakespeare's historical plays, which are rather chronicles represented than tragedies, and all double action of plays. As to avoid a satire upon others, I will make bold with my own *Marriage a-la-Mode*, where there are manifestly two actions, not depending on one another: but in *Oedipus* there cannot properly be said to be two actions, because the love of Adrastus and Eurydice has a necessary dependence on the principal design, into which it is woven. The natural reason of rule is plain; for two different independent actions distract the attention and concernment of the audience, and consequently destroy the intention of the poet: if his business be to move terror and pity, and one of his actions be comical, the other tragical, the former will divert the people, and utterly make void his greater purpose. Therefore, as in perspective, so in tragedy, there must be a point of sight in which all the lines terminate; otherwise the eye wanders, and the work is false. This was the practice of the Grecian stage. But Terence made an innovation in the Roman: all his plays have double actions; for it was his custom to translate two Greek comedies, and to weave them into one of his, yet so that both the actions were comical, and one was principal, the other but secondary or subservient. And this has obtained on the English stage, to give us the pleasure of variety.

As the action ought to be one, it ought, as such, to have order in it, that is, to have a natural beginning, a middle, and an end. A natural beginning, says Aristotle, is that which could not necessarily have been placed after another thing, and so of the rest. This consideration will arraign all plays after the new model of Spanish plots, where accident is heaped upon accident, and that which is first might as reasonably be last: an inconvenience not to be remedied but by making one accident naturally produce another, otherwise 'tis a farce and not a play. Of this nature is the *Slighted*

*Maid*,[5] where there is no scene in the first act which might not by as good reason be in the fifth. And if the action ought to be one, the tragedy ought likewise to conclude with the action of it. Thus in *Mustapha*,[6] the play should naturally have ended with the death of Zanger, and not have given us the grace cup after dinner of Solyman's divorce from Roxolana.

The following properties of the action are so easy that they need not my explaining. It ought to be great, and to consist of great persons, to distinguish it from comedy, where the action is trivial, and the persons of inferior rank. The last quality of the action is that it ought to be probable, as well as admirable and great. 'Tis not necessary that there should be historical truth in it; but always necessary that there should be a likeness of truth, something that is more than barely possible, *probable* being that which succeeds or happens oftener than it misses. To invent therefore a probability, and to make it wonderful, is the most difficult undertaking in the art of poetry; for that which is not wonderful is not great; and that which is not probable will not delight a reasonable audience. This action, thus described, must be represented and not told, to distinguish dramatic poetry from epic: but I hasten to the end or scope of tragedy, which is to rectify or purge our passions, fear and pity.

To instruct delightfully is the general end of all poetry. Philosophy instructs, but it performs its work by precept: which is not delightful, or not so delightful as example. To purge the passions by example is therefore the particular instruction which belongs to tragedy. Rapin, a judicious critic, has observed from Aristotle that pride and want of commiseration are the most predominant vices in mankind: therefore, to cure us of these two, the inventors of tragedy have chosen to work upon two other passions, which are fear and pity. We are wrought to fear by their setting before our eyes some terrible example of misfortune, which happened to persons of the highest quality; for such an action demonstrates to us that no condition is privileged from the turns of fortune; this must of necessity cause terror in us, and consequently abate our pride. But when we see that the most virtuous, as well as the greatest, are not exempt from

5. By Sir Robert Stapylton (1663).
6. By Roger Boyle, Earl of Orrery (first performed in 1665).

such misfortunes, that consideration moves pity in us, and insensibly works us to be helpful to, and tender over, the distressed, which is the noblest and most god-like of moral virtues. Here 'tis observable that it is absolutely necessary to make a man virtuous, if we desire he should be pitied: we lament not, but detest, a wicked man; we are glad when we behold his crimes are punished, and that poetical justice[7] is done upon him. Euripides was censured by the critics of his time for making his chief characters too wicked: for example, Phaedra, though she loved her son-in-law with reluctancy, and that it was a curse upon her family for offending Venus, yet was thought too ill a pattern for the stage. Shall we therefore banish all characters of villainy? I confess I am not of that opinion; but it is necessary that the hero of the play be not a villain; that is, the characters which should move our pity ought to have virtuous inclinations, and degrees of moral goodness in them. As for a perfect character of virtue, it never was in nature, and therefore there can be no imitation of it; but there are allays of frailty to be allowed for the chief persons, yet so that the good which is in them shall outweigh the bad, and consequently leave room for punishment on the one side, and pity on the other.

After all, if anyone will ask me whether a tragedy cannot be made upon any other grounds than those of exciting pity and terror in us, Bossu,[8] the best of modern critics, answers thus in general: that all excellent arts, and particularly that of poetry, have been invented and brought to perfection by men of a transcendent genius; and that therefore they who practice afterwards the same arts are obliged to tread in their footsteps, and to search in their writings the foundation of them; for it is not just that new rules should destroy the authority of the old. But Rapin writes more particularly thus:[9] that no passions in a story are so proper to move our concernment as fear and pity; and that it is from our concernment we receive our pleasure, is undoubted; when the soul becomes agitated with fear for one character, or hope for another, then it is that we are pleased in tragedy by the interest which we take in their adventures.

7. A phrase first coined by Rymer in *The Tragedies of the Last Age*.
8. Le Bossu, author of *Traité du poème épique* (1675).
9. In *Réflexions sur la poétique d'Aristote* (1674).

Here, therefore, the general answer may be given to the first question, how far we ought to imitate Shakespeare and Fletcher in their plots: namely, that we ought to follow them so far only as they have copied the excellencies of those who invented and brought to perfection dramatic poetry: those things only excepted which religion, customs of countries, idioms of languages, etc., have altered in the superstructures, but not in the foundation of the design.

How defective Shakespeare and Fletcher have been in all their plots, Mr. Rymer has discovered in his criticisms: neither can we who follow them be excused from the same or greater errors; which are the more unpardonable in us, because we want their beauties to countervail our faults. The best of their designs, the most approaching to antiquity, and the most conducing to move pity, is the *King and No King*; which, if the farce of Bessus were thrown away, is of that inferior sort of tragedies which end with a prosperous event. 'Tis probably derived from the story of Oedipus, with the character of Alexander the Great, in his extravagancies, given to Arbaces. The taking of this play, amongst many others, I cannot wholly ascribe to the excellency of the action; for I find it moving when it is read: 'tis true, the faults of the plot are so evidently proved that they can no longer be denied. The beauties of it must therefore lie either in the lively touches of the passion: or we must conclude, as I think we may, that even in imperfect plots there are less degrees of nature, by which some faint emotions of pity and terror are raised in us: as a less engine will raise a less proportion of weight, though not so much as one of Archimedes' making; for nothing can move our nature, but by some natural reason, which works upon passions. And since we acknowledge the effect, there must be something in the cause.

The difference between Shakespeare and Fletcher in their plotting seems to be this: that Shakespeare generally moves more terror, and Fletcher more compassion. For the first had a more masculine, a bolder and more fiery genius; the second, a more soft and womanish. In the mechanic beauties of the plot, which are the observation of the three unities, time, place, and action, they are both deficient; but Shakespeare most. Ben Jonson reformed those errors in his comedies, yet one of Shakespeare's was regular before him; which is, *The Merry Wives of Windsor*. For what remains concerning the design, you are to be referred to our English critic. That method which he has prescribed to raise it from mistake, or ignorance of the crime, is certainly the best, though 'tis not the only: for amongst all the tragedies of Sophocles, there is but one, *Oedipus*, which is wholly built after that model.

After the plot, which is the foundation of the play, the next thing to which we ought to apply our judgment is the manners, for now the poet comes to work above ground: the ground-work indeed is that which is most necessary, as that upon which depends the firmness of the whole fabric; yet it strikes not the eye so much as the beauties or imperfections of the manners, the thoughts, and the expressions.

The first rule which Bossu prescribes to the writer of an heroic poem, and which holds too by the same reason in all dramatic poetry, is to make the moral of the work, that is, to lay down to yourself what that precept of morality shall be, which you would insinuate into the people; as namely, Homer's (which I have copied in my *Conquest of Granada*) was, that union preserves a commonwealth, and discord destroys it; Sophocles, in his *Oedipus*, that no man is to be accounted happy before his death. 'Tis the moral that directs the whole action of the play to one center; and that action or fable is the example built upon the moral, which confirms the truth of it to our experience: when the fable is designed, then and not before, the persons are to be introduced with their manners, characters, and passions.

The manners in a poem are understood to be those inclinations, whether natural or acquired, which move and carry us to actions, good, bad, or indifferent, in a play; or which incline the persons to such or such actions. I have anticipated part of this discourse already, in declaring that a poet ought not to make the manners perfectly good in his best persons; but neither are they to be more wicked in any of his characters than necessity requires. To produce a villain, without other reason than a natural inclination to villainy is, in poetry, to produce an effect without a cause; and to make him more a villain than he has just reason to be, is to make an effect which is stronger than the cause.

The manners arise from many causes; and are either distinguished by complexion, as choleric and phlegmatic, or by the differences of age or sex, of climates, or quality of the persons, or their present condition. They are likewise to be gathered from the several virtues, vices, or passions, and many other commonplaces which a poet must be supposed to have learned from natural philosophy, ethics, and history; of all which whosoever is ignorant, does not deserve the name of poet.

But as the manners are useful in this art, they may be all comprised under these general heads: first, they must be apparent; that is, in every character of the play, some inclinations of the person must appear: and these are shown in the actions and discourse. Secondly, the manners must be suitable, or agreeing to the persons; that is, to the age, sex, dignity, and the other general heads of manners: thus, when a poet has given the dignity of a king to one of his persons, in all his actions and speeches, that person must discover majesty, magnanimity, and jealousy of power, because these are suitable to the general manners of a king. The third property of manners is resemblance; and this is founded upon the particular characters of men, as we have them delivered to us by relation or history; that is, when a poet has the known character of this or that man before him, he is bound to represent him such, at least not contrary to that which fame has reported him to have been. Thus, it is not a poet's choice to make Ulysses choleric, or Achilles patient, because Homer has described 'em quite otherwise. Yet this is a rock on which ignorant writers daily split; and the absurdity is as monstrous as if a painter should draw a coward running from a battle, and tell us it was the picture of Alexander the Great.

The last property of manners is that they be constant and equal, that is, maintained the same through the whole design: thus, when Virgil had once given the name of *pious* to Æneas, he was bound to show him such, in all his words and actions through the whole poem. All these properties Horace has hinted to a judicious observer: "1. you must mark the manners of each age; 2. or follow tradition; 3. or create your own convention; 4. let each character remain constant and consistent with itself." [10]

10. "*1. notandi sunt tibi mores; 2. aut famam sequere; 3. aut sibi convenientia finge; 4. servetur ad imum, qualis ab incepto processerit, et sibi constet*" (*Ars poetica*, ll. 156, 119, 126–127).

From the manners, the characters of persons are derived; for indeed the characters are no other than the inclinations, as they appear in the several persons of the poem; a character being thus defined, that which distinguishes one man from another. Not to repeat the same things over again which have been said of the manners, I will only add what is necessary here. A character, or that which distinguishes one man from all others, cannot be supposed to consist of one particular virtue, or vice, or passion only; but 'tis a composition of qualities which are not contrary to one another in the same person; thus the same man may be liberal and valiant, but not liberal and covetous; so in a comical character, or humour (which is an inclination to this or that particular folly), Falstaff is a liar, and a coward, a glutton, and a buffoon, because all these qualities may agree in the same man; yet it is still to be observed that one virtue, vice, and passion ought to be shown in every man, as predominant over all the rest; as covetousness in Crassus, love of his country in Brutus; and the same in characters which are feigned.

The chief character or hero in a tragedy, as I have already shown, ought in prudence to be such a man who has so much more in him of virtue than of vice, that he may be left amiable to the audience, which otherwise cannot have any concernment for his sufferings; and 'tis on this one character that the pity and terror must be principally, if not wholly, founded—a rule which is extremely necessary, and which none of the critics that I know have fully enough discovered to us. For terror and compassion work but weakly when they are divided into many persons. If Creon had been the chief character in *Oedipus*, there had neither been terror nor compassion moved; but only detestation of the man and joy for his punishment; if Adrastus and Eurydice had been made more appearing characters, then the pity had been divided, and lessened on the part of Oedipus: but making Oedipus the best and bravest person, and even Jocasta but an underpart to him, his virtues and the punishment of his fatal crime drew both the pity and the terror to himself.

By what had been said of the manners, it will be easy for a reasonable man to judge whether the characters be truly or falsely drawn in a tragedy; for if there be no manners appearing in the characters, no concernment for the persons can be raised; no pity or horror can be moved, but by vice or virtue; therefore, without them, no person can have any business in the play. If the inclinations be obscure, 'tis a sign the poet is in the dark, and knows not what manner of man he presents to you; and consequently you can have no idea, or very imperfect, of that man; nor can judge what resolutions he ought to take; or what words or actions are proper for him. Most comedies made up of accidents or adventures are liable to fall into this error; and tragedies with many turns are subject to it; for the manners never can be evident where the surprises of fortune take up all the business of the stage; and where the poet is more in pain to tell you what happened to such a man than what he was. 'Tis one of the excellencies of Shakespeare that the manners of his persons are generally apparent, and you see their bent and inclinations. Fletcher comes far short of him in this, as indeed he does almost in everything: there are but glimmerings of manners in most of his comedies, which run upon adventures: and in his tragedies, *Rollo*, *Otto*, the *King and No King*, *Melantius*,[11] and many others of his best, are but pictures shown you in the twilight; you know not whether they resemble vice or virtue, and they are either good, bad, or indifferent, as the present scene requires it. But of all poets, this commendation is to be given to Ben Jonson, that the manners even of the most inconsiderable persons in his plays are everywhere apparent.

By considering the second quality of manners, which is that they be suitable to the age, quality, country, dignity, etc., of the character, we may likewise judge whether a poet has followed nature. In this kind, Sophocles and Euripides have more excelled among the Greeks than Æschylus; and Terence more than Plautus among the Romans. Thus Sophocles gives to Oedipus the true qualities of a king, in both those plays which bear his name; but in the latter, which is the *Oedipus Colonæus*, he lets fall on purpose his tragic style; his hero speaks not in the arbitrary tone, but remembers, in the softness of his complaints, that he is an unfortunate blind old man, that he is banished from his country, and persecuted by his next relations. The present French poets are generally accused that wheresoever they lay the scene, or in whatsoever age, the manners of their

11. Otto is Rollo's brother; Melantius is a character in *The Maid's Tragedy*.

heroes are wholly French. Racine's Bajazet is bred at Constantinople, but his civilities are conveyed to him, by some secret passage, from Versailles into the Seraglio. But our Shakespeare, having ascribed to Henry the Fourth the character of a king and of a father, gives him the perfect manners of each relation, when either he transacts with his son or with his subjects. Fletcher, on the other side, gives neither to Arbaces, nor to his King in the *Maid's Tragedy*, the qualities which are suitable to a monarch; though he may be excused a little in the latter, for the King there is not uppermost in the character; 'tis the lover of Evadne, who is King only in a second consideration; and though he be unjust, and has other faults which shall be nameless, yet he is not the hero of the play. 'Tis true, we find him a lawful prince (though I never heard of any King that was in Rhodes), and therefore Mr. Rymer's criticism stands good; that he should not be shown in so vicious a character. Sophocles has been more judicious in his *Antigona*; for though he represents in Creon a bloody prince, yet he makes him not a lawful king, but an usurper, and Antigona herself is the heroine of the tragedy. But when Philaster wounds Arethusa and the boy; and Perigot his mistress, in the *Faithful Shepherdess*, both these are contrary to the character of manhood. Nor is Valentinian managed much better, for though Fletcher has taken his picture truly, and shown him as he was, an effeminate, voluptuous man, yet he has forgotten that he was an Emperor, and has given him none of those royal marks which ought to appear in a lawful successor of the throne. If it be inquired what Fletcher should have done on this occasion: ought he not to have represented Valentinian as he was? Bossu shall answer this question for me, by an instance of the like nature: Mauritius, the Greek Emperor, was a prince far surpassing Valentinian, for he was endued with many kingly virtues; he was religious, merciful, and valiant, but withal he was noted of extreme covetousness, a vice which is contrary to the character of a hero, or a prince: therefore, says the critic, that emperor was no fit person to be represented in a tragedy, unless his good qualities were only to be shown, and his covetousness (which sullied them all) were slurred over by the artifice of the poet.[12] To return once more to Shakespeare: no man

12. *Traité du poème épique*, IV. vii.

ever drew so many characters, or generally distinguished 'em better from one another, excepting only Jonson. I will instance but in one, to show the copiousness of his invention: 'tis that of Caliban, or the Monster in the *Tempest*. He seems there to have created a person which was not in nature, a boldness which at first sight would appear intolerable; for he makes him a species of himself, begotten by an incubus on a witch; but this, as I have elsewhere proved, is not wholly beyond the bounds of credibility, at least the vulgar still believe it. We have the separated notions of a spirit, and of a witch (and spirits, according to Plato, are vested with a subtle body; according to some of his followers, have different sexes); therefore, as from the distinct apprehensions of a horse, and of a man, imagination has formed a centaur; so from those of an incubus and a sorceress, Shakespeare has produced his monster. Whether or no his generation can be defended, I leave to philosophy; but of this I am certain, that the poet has most judiciously furnished him with a person, a language, and a character, which will suit him, both by father's and mother's side: he has all the discontents and malice of a witch, and of a devil, besides a convenient proportion of the deadly sins; gluttony, sloth, and lust are manifest; the dejectedness of a slave is likewise given him, and the ignorance of one bred up in a desert island. His person is monstrous, as he is the product of unnatural lust; and his language is as hobgoblin as his person; in all things he is distinguished from other mortals. The characters of Fletcher are poor and narrow, in comparison of Shakespeare's; I remember not one which is not borrowed from him; unless you will except that strange mixture of a man in the *King and No King*; so that in this part Shakespeare is generally worth our imitation; and to imitate Fletcher is but to copy after him who was a copier.

Under this general head of manners, the passions are naturally included, as belonging to the characters. I speak not of pity and of terror, which are to be moved in the audience by the plot; but of anger, hatred, love, ambition, jealousy, revenge, etc., as they are shown in this or that person of the play. To describe these naturally, and to move them artfully, is one of the greatest commendations which can be given to a poet: to write pathetically, says Longinus, cannot proceed but from a lofty genius. A poet must be born with this quality; yet, unless he help himself by an acquired knowledge of the passions, what they are in their own nature, and by what springs they are to be moved, he will be subject either to raise them where they ought not to be raised, or not to raise them by the just degrees of nature, or to amplify them beyond the natural bounds, or not to observe the crisis and turns of them, in their cooling and decay: all which errors proceed from want of judgment in the poet, and from being unskilled in the principles of moral philosophy. Nothing is more frequent in a fanciful writer than to foil himself by not managing his strength; therefore, as in a wrestler, there is first required some measure of force, a well-knit body, and active limbs, without which all instruction would be vain; yet, these being granted, if he want the skill which is necessary to a wrestler, he shall make but small advantage of his natural robustuousness: so, in a poet, his inborn vehemence and force of spirit will only run him out of breath the sooner, if it be not supported by the help of art. The roar of passion indeed may please an audience, three parts of which are ignorant enough to think all is moving which is noise, and it may stretch the lungs of an ambitious actor, who will die upon the spot for a thundering clap; but it will move no other passion than indignation and contempt from judicious men. Longinus, whom I have hitherto followed, continues thus: *If the passions be artfully employed, the discourse becomes vehement and lofty: if otherwise, there is nothing more ridiculous than a great passion out of season:* and to this purpose he animadverts severely upon Æschylus, who writ nothing in cold blood, but was always in a rapture, and in fury with his audience:[13] the inspiration was still upon him, he was ever tearing it upon the tripos;[14] or (to run off as madly as he does, from one similitude to another) he was always at high flood of passion, even in the dead ebb and lowest water-mark of the scene. He who would raise the passion of a judicious audience, says a learned critic, must be sure to take his hearers along with him; if they be in a calm, 'tis in vain for him to be in a huff: he must move them by degrees,

13. *On the Sublime*, iii.
14. A reference to the tripod at Delphi on which the priestess of Apollo delivered her raving oracles.

and kindle with 'em; otherwise he will be in danger of setting his own heap of stubble on a fire, and of burning out by himself without warming the company that stand about him. They who would justify the madness of poetry from the authority of Aristotle have mistaken the text, and consequently the interpretation: I imagine it to be false read, where he says of poetry that it is εὐφυοῦς ἤ μανικοῦ, that it had always somewhat in it either of a genius, or of a madman. 'Tis more probable that the original ran thus, that poetry was εὐφυοῦς οὐ μανικοῦ, that it belongs to a witty man, but not to a madman.[15] Thus then the passions, as they are considered simply and in themselves, suffer violence when they are perpetually maintained at the same height; for what melody can be made on that instrument, all whose strings are screwed up at first to their utmost stretch, and to the same sound? But this is not the worst: for the characters likewise bear a part in the general calamity, if you consider the passions as embodied in them; for it follows of necessity that no man can be distinguished from another by his discourse, when every man is ranting, swaggering, and exclaiming with the same excess: as if it were the only business of all the characters to contend with each other for the prize at Billingsgate; or that the scene of the tragedy lay in Bet'lem.[16] Suppose the poet should intend this man to be choleric, and that man to be patient; yet when they are confounded in the writing, you cannot distinguish them from one another: for the man who was called patient and tame is only so before he speaks; but let his clack be set a-going, and he shall tongue it as impetuously, and as loudly, as the errantest hero in the play. By this means, the characters are only distinct in name; but, in reality, all the men and women in the play are the same person. No man should pretend to write who cannot temper his fancy with his judgment: nothing is more dangerous to a raw horseman than a hot-mouthed jade without a curb.

'Tis necessary therefore for a poet who would concern an audience by describing of a passion, first to prepare it, and not to rush upon it all at once. Ovid has judiciously shown the difference of these two ways, in the speeches of Ajax and Ulysses: Ajax, from the very

15. Aristotle, *Poetics*, xvii.
16. Bedlam, a London hospital for the insane.

beginning, breaks out into his exclamations, and is swearing by his Maker, "'By Jupiter,' he cried."[17] Ulysses, on the contrary, prepares his audience with all the submissiveness he can practice, and all the calmness of a reasonable man; he found his judges in a tranquillity of spirit, and therefore set out leisurely and softly with 'em, till he had warmed 'em by degrees; and then he began to mend his pace, and to draw them along with his own impetuousness: yet so managing his breath, that it might not fail him at his need, and reserving his utmost proofs of ability even to the last. The success, you see, was answerable; for the crowd only applauded the speech of Ajax:

and the applause of the crowd followed his closing words.[18]

But the judges awarded the prize for which they contended to Ulysses:

the assembly was very moved; and the power of eloquence was revealed, and the skillful orator carried off the hero's arms.[19]

The next necessary rule is to put nothing into the discourse which may hinder your moving of the passions. Too many accidents, as I have said, encumber the poet, as much as the arms of Saul did David; for the variety of passions which they produce are ever crossing and jostling each other out of the way. He who treats of joy and grief together is in a fair way of causing neither of those effects. There is yet another obstacle to be removed, which is pointed wit, and sentences affected out of season; these are nothing of kin to the violence of passion: no man is at leisure to make sentences and similes when his soul is in an agony. I the rather name this fault that it may serve to mind me of my former errors; neither will I spare myself, but give an example of this kind from my *Indian Emperor*.

17. *"agimus, proh Jupiter, inquit"* (Metamorphoses, xiii. 5).
18.       *vulgique secutum*
  *ultima mumur erat.*
        *Ibid.,* 123.
19. *mota manus procerum est; et quid facundia posset*
  *tum patuit, fortisque viri tulit arma disertus.*
        *Ibid.,* 282–283.

Montezuma, pursued by his enemies, and seeking sanctuary, stands parleying without the fort, and describing his danger to Cydaria, in a simile of six lines:

> As on the sands the frighted traveller
> Sees the high seas come rolling from afar, etc.[20]

My Indian potentate was well skilled in the sea for an inland prince, and well improved since the first act, when he sent his son to discover it. The image had not been amiss from another man, at another time: "but not now, in this place";[21] he destroyed the concernment which the audience might otherwise have had for him; for they could not think the danger near when he had the leisure to invent a simile.

If Shakespeare be allowed, as I think he must, to have made his characters distinct, it will easily be inferred that he understood the nature of the passions: because it has been proved already that confused passions make undistinguishable characters. Yet I cannot deny that he has his failings; but they are not so much in the passions themselves as in his manner of expression: he often obscures his meaning by his words, and sometimes makes it unintelligible. I will not say of so great a poet that he distinguished not the blown puffy style from true sublimity; but I may venture to maintain that the fury of his fancy often transported him beyond the bounds of judgment, either in coining of new words and phrases, or racking words which were in use into the violence of a catachresis.[22] 'Tis not that I would explode[23] the use of metaphors from passions, for Longinus thinks 'em necessary to raise it: but to use 'em at every word, to say nothing without a metaphor, a simile, an image, or description, is I doubt to smell a little too strongly of the buskin. I must be forced to give an example of expressing passion figuratively; but that I may do it with respect to Shakespeare, it shall not be taken from anything of his: 'tis an exclamation against Fortune, quoted in his *Hamlet*, but written by some other poet:

20. Act V.
21. "*sed nunc non erat hisce locus*" (*Ars poetica*, l. 19).
22. A misuse of terms.
23. Banish, reject.

> Out, out, thou strumpet Fortune! all you gods,
> In general synod, take away her power;
> Break all the spokes and felleys from her wheel,
> And bowl the round nave down the hill of Heav'n,
> As low as to the fiends.

And immediately after, speaking of Hecuba, when Priam was killed before her eyes:

> The mobbled queen ran up and down,
> Threatening the flame with bisson rheum; a clout
>     about that head
> Where late the diadem stood; and for a robe,
> About her lank and all o'er-teemed loins,
> A blanket in th' alarm of fear caught up.
> Who this had seen, with tongue in venom steep'd
> 'Gainst Fortune's state would treason have
>     pronounced;
> But if the gods themselves did see her then,
> When she saw Pyrrhus make malicious sport
> In mincing with his sword her husband's limbs,
> The instant burst of clamour that she made
> (Unless things mortal move them not at all)
> Would have made milch the burning eyes of Heaven,
> And passion in the gods.[24]

What a pudder is here kept in raising the expression of trifling thoughts! Would not a man have thought that the poet had been bound prentice to a wheelwright, for his first rant? and had followed a ragman for the clout and blanket, in the second? Fortune is painted on a wheel, and therefore the writer, in a rage, will have poetical justice down upon every member of that engine: after this execution, he bowls the nave down hill, from Heaven to the fiends (an unreasonable long mark, a man would think); 'tis well there are no solid orbs to stop it in the way, or no element of fire to consume it: but when it came to the earth, it must be monstrous heavy, to break ground as low as to the center. His making milch the burning eyes of Heaven was a pretty tolerable flight too: and I think no man ever drew milk out of eyes before him: yet to make the wonder

24. *Hamlet*, II, ii, 515–519, 524, 528–541.

greater, these eyes were burning. Such a sight indeed were enough to have raised passion in the gods; but to excuse the effects of it, he tells you perhaps they did not see it. Wise men would be glad to find a little sense couched under all those pompous words; for bombast is commonly the delight of that audience which loves poetry, but understands it not: and as commonly has been the practice of those writers who, not being able to infuse a natural passion into the mind, have made it their business to ply the ears and to stun their judges by the noise. But Shakespeare does not often thus; for the passions in his scene between Brutus and Cassius are extremely natural, the thoughts are such as arise from the matter, and the expression of 'em not viciously figurative. I cannot leave this subject before I do justice to that divine poet by giving you one of his passionate descriptions: 'tis of Richard the Second when he was deposed, and led in triumph through the streets of London by Henry of Bolingbroke: the painting of it is so lively, and the words so moving, that I have scarce read anything comparable to it in any other language. Suppose you have seen already the fortunate usurper passing through the crowd, and followed by the shouts and acclamations of the people; and now behold King Richard entering upon the scene: consider the wretchedness of his condition, and his carriage in it; and refrain from pity if you can:

> As in a theater, the eyes of men,
> After a well-graced actor leaves the stage,
> Are idly bent on him that enters next,
> Thinking his prattle to be tedious:
> Even so, or with much more contempt, men's eyes
> Did scowl on Richard: no man cried, God save him:
> No joyful tongue gave him his welcome home,
> But dust was thrown upon his sacred head,
> Which with such gentle sorrow he shook off,
> His face still combating with tears and smiles
> (The badges of his grief and patience),
> That had not God (for some strong purpose) steel'd
> The hearts of men, they must perforce have melted,
> And barbarism itself have pitied him.[25]

25. *Richard II*, V, ii, 23–36.

To speak justly of this whole matter: 'tis neither height of thought that is discommended, nor pathetic vehemence, nor any nobleness of expression in its proper place; but 'tis a false measure of all these, something which is like 'em, and is not them; 'tis the Bristol-stone,[26] which appears like a diamond; 'tis an extravagant thought, instead of a sublime one; 'tis roaring madness, instead of vehemence; and a sound of words, instead of sense. If Shakespeare were stripped of all the bombast in his passions, and dressed in the most vulgar words, we should find the beauties of his thoughts remaining; if his embroideries were burnt down, there would still be silver at the bottom of the melting-pot: but I fear (at least let me fear it for myself) that we who ape his sounding words have nothing of his thought, but are all outside; there is not so much as a dwarf within our giant's clothes. Therefore, let not Shakespeare suffer for our sakes; 'tis our fault, who succeed him in an age which is more refined, if we imitate him so ill that we copy his failings only, and make a virtue of that in our writings which in his was an imperfection.

For what remains, the excellency of that poet was, as I have said, in the more manly passions; Fletcher's in the softer: Shakespeare writ better betwixt man and man; Fletcher, betwixt man and woman: consequently, the one described friendship better; the other love: yet Shakespeare taught Fletcher to write love: and Juliet, and Desdemona, are originals. 'Tis true, the scholar had the softer soul; but the master had the kinder. Friendship is both a virtue and a passion essentially; love is a passion only in its nature, and is not a virtue but by accident: good nature makes friendship, but effeminacy love. Shakespeare had an universal mind, which comprehended all characters and passions; Fletcher a more confined and limited: for though he treated love in perfection, yet honor, ambition, revenge, and generally all the stronger passions, he either touched not, or not masterly. To conclude all, he was a limb of Shakespeare.

I had intended to have proceeded to the last property of manners, which is that they must be constant, and the characters maintained the same from the beginning to the end; and from thence to have proceeded to the thoughts and expressions suitable to a tragedy:

26. A rock crystal.

but I will first see how this will relish with the age. 'Tis, I confess, but cursorily written; yet the judgment which is given here is generally founded upon experience: but because many men are shocked at the name of rules, as if they were a kind of magisterial prescription upon poets, I will conclude with the words of Rapin, in his reflections on Aristotle's work of poetry: "If the rules be well considered, we shall find them to be made only to reduce nature into method, to trace her step by step, and not to suffer the least mark of her to escape us: 'tis only by these that probability in fiction is maintained, which is the soul of poetry. They are founded upon good sense, and sound reason, rather than on authority; for though Aristotole and Horace are produced, yet no man must argue that what they write is true because they writ it; but 'tis evident, by the ridiculous mistakes and gross absurdities which have been made by those poets who have taken their fancy only for their guide, that if this fancy be not regulated, 'tis a mere caprice, and utterly incapable to produce a reasonable and judicious poem." [27]

"A Preface Containing the Grounds of Criticism in Tragedy," in *Troilus and Cressida* (London: printed for Jacob Tonson, 1679), sigs. A4v–b3v.

27. *Réflexions*, xii.

# Preface to
## *Fables Ancient and Modern, Translated into Verse from Homer, Ovid, Boccaccio, and Chaucer, with Original Poems* (1700)

*The preface to the* Fables *is Dryden's most personal critical essay; it not only reveals him, it is about him. His temperament, his controversies, and above all, his responses to literature are the subject of the essay. For he writes not so much about literature as about himself in relation to literature; and it is through this relationship, imaginatively created for us, that we come to see and understand the works and authors he discusses. The essay is thus personal in the most rewarding sense, for, as in most great criticism, Dryden's re-creation of his own experience is an enlargement of ours.*

'Tis with a poet as with a man who designs to build, and is very exact, as he supposes, in casting up the cost beforehand; but, generally speaking, he is mistaken in his account, and reckons short of the expense he first intended: he alters his mind as the work proceeds, and will have this or that convenience more, of which he had not thought when he began. So has it happened to me; I have built a house where I intended but a lodge; yet with better success than a certain nobleman, who, beginning with a dog-kennel, never lived to finish the palace he had contrived.

From translating the first of Homer's *Iliads* (which I intended as an essay to the whole work), I proceeded to the translation of the twelfth book of Ovid's *Metamorphoses*, because it contains, among other things, the causes, the beginning, and ending, of the Trojan War. Here I ought in reason to have stopped; but the speeches of Ajax and Ulysses lying next in my way, I could not balk 'em. When I had compassed them, I was so taken with the former part of the fifteenth book (which is the masterpiece of the whole *Metamorphoses*), that I enjoined myself the pleasing task of rendering it into English. And now I found, by the number of my verses, that they began to swell into a little volume; which gave me an occasion of looking backward on some beauties of my author, in his former books: there occurred to me the Hunting of the Boar, Cinyras and Myrrha, the good-natured story of Baucis and Philemon, with the rest, which I hope I have translated closely enough, and given them the same turn of verse which they had in the original; and this, I may say without vanity, is not the talent of every poet. He who has arrived the nearest to it, is the ingenious and learned Sandys, the best versifier of the former age; if I may properly call it by that name, which was the former part of this concluding century. For Spenser and Fairfax both flourished in the reign of Queen Elizabeth; great masters in our language, and who saw much farther into the beauties of our numbers than those who immediately followed them. Milton was the poetical son of Spenser, and Mr. Waller of Fairfax; for we have our lineal descents and clans as well as other families: Spenser more than once insinuates that the soul of Chaucer was transfused into his body; and that he was begotten by him two hundred years after his decease. Milton has acknowledged to me that Spenser was his original; and many besides myself have heard our famous Waller own that he derived the harmony of his numbers from the *Godfrey of Bulloign*, which was turned into English by Mr. Fairfax.

But to return: having done with Ovid for this time, it came into my mind that our old English poet, Chaucer, in many things resembled him, and that with no disadvantage on the side of the modern author, as I shall endeavor to prove when I compare them; and as I am, and always have been, studious to promote the honor of my native country, so I soon resolved to put their merits to the trial, by turning some of the *Canterbury Tales* into our language, as it is now refined; for by this means, both the poets being set in the same light and dressed in the same English habit, story to be compared with story, a certain judgment may be made betwixt them by the reader, without obtruding my opinion on him: or, if I seem partial to my countryman and predecessor in the laurel, the friends of antiquity are not few; and besides many of the learned, Ovid has almost all the beaux, and the whole fair sex, his declared patrons. Perhaps I have assumed somewhat more to myself than they allow me, because I have adventured to sum up the evidence; but the readers are the jury, and their privilege remains entire to decide according to the merits of the cause: or, if they please, to bring it to another hearing before some other court. In the meantime, to follow the thread of my discourse (as thoughts, according to Mr. Hobbes, have always some connection),[1] so from Chaucer I was led to think on Boccaccio, who was not only his contemporary, but also pursued the same studies; wrote novels in prose, and many works in verse; particularly is said to have invented the octave rhyme, or stanza of eight lines, which ever since has been maintained by the practice of all Italian writers who are, or at least assume the title of, heroic poets. He and Chaucer, among other things, had this in common, that they refined their mother-tongues; but with this difference, that Dante had begun to file their language, at least in verse, before the time of Boccaccio, who likewise received no little help from his master Petrarch; but the reformation of their prose was wholly owing to Boccaccio himself, who is yet the standard of purity in the Italian tongue; though many of his phrases are become obsolete, as in process of time it must needs happen. Chaucer (as you have formerly been told by our learned Mr. Rymer[2]) first adorned and amplified our barren tongue from the Provençal, which was then the most polished of all the modern languages; but this subject has been copiously treated by that great critic, who deserves no little commendation from us his countrymen.

For these reasons of time, and resemblance of genius, in Chaucer and Boccaccio, I resolved to join them in my present work; to which I have added some original papers of my own, which whether they

1. Hobbes developed a theory of association of ideas in the *Leviathan* (1651), I. iii.

2. *A Short View of Tragedy* (1693), vi.

are equal or inferior to my other poems, an author is the most improper judge; and therefore I leave them wholly to the mercy of the reader. I will hope the best, that they will not be condemned; but if they should, I have the excuse of an old gentleman who, mounting on horseback before some ladies, when I was present, got up somewhat heavily, but desired of the fair spectators that they would count fourscore and eight before they judged him. By the mercy of God, I am already come within twenty years of his number; a cripple in my limbs, but what decays are in my mind the reader must determine. I think myself as vigorous as ever in the faculties of my soul, excepting only my memory, which is not impaired to any great degree; and if I lose not more of it, I have no great reason to complain. What judgment I had, increases rather than diminishes; and thoughts, such as they are, come crowding in so fast upon me that my only difficulty is to choose or to reject, to run them into verse or to give them the other harmony of prose: I have so long studied and practiced both that they are grown into a habit, and become familiar to me. In short, though I may lawfully plead some part of the old gentleman's excuse, yet I will reserve it till I think I have greater need, and ask no grains of allowance for the faults of this my present work, but those which are given of course to human frailty. I will not trouble my reader with the shortness of time in which I writ it, or the several intervals of sickness. They who think too well of their own performances are apt to boast in their prefaces how little time their works have cost them, and what other business of more importance interfered; but the reader will be as apt to ask the question, why they allowed not a longer time to make their works more perfect? and why they had so despicable an opinion of their judges as to thrust their indigested stuff upon them, as if they deserved no better?

With this account of my present undertaking, I conclude the first part of this discourse: in the second part, as at a second sitting, though I alter not the draught, I must touch the same features over again, and change the dead-coloring[3] of the whole. In general, I will only say that I have written nothing which savors of immorality or profaneness; at least, I am not conscious to myself of any such

3. The first, or preparatory, layer of color in a painting.

intention. If there happen to be found an irreverent expression, or a thought too wanton, they are crept into my verses through my inadvertency: if the searchers find any in the cargo, let them be staved or forfeited, like counterbanded goods; at least, let their authors be answerable for them, as being but imported merchandise, and not of my own manufacture. On the other side, I have endeavored to choose such fables, both ancient and modern, as contain in each of them some instructive moral, which I could prove by induction, but the way is tedious; and they leap foremost into sight without the reader's trouble of looking after them. I wish I could affirm, with a safe conscience, that I had taken the same care in all my former writings; for it must be owned, that supposing verses are never so beautiful or pleasing, yet if they contain anything which shocks religion or good manners, they are at best what Horace says of good numbers without good sense, "verses without thought, and melodious trifles." [4] Thus far, I hope, I am right in court, without renouncing to my other right of self-defense, where I have been wrongfully accused, and my sense wire-drawn into blasphemy or bawdry, as it has often been by a religious lawyer, [5] in a late pleading against the stage; in which he mixes truth with falsehood, and has not forgotten the old rule of calumniating strongly, that something may remain.

I resume the thread of my discourse with the first of my translations, which was the first *Iliad* of Homer. If it shall please God to give me longer life, and moderate health, my intentions are to translate the whole *Ilias*; provided still that I meet with those encouragements from the public which may enable me to proceed in my undertaking with some cheerfulness. And this I dare assure the world beforehand, that I have found, by trial, Homer a more pleasing task than Virgil (though I say not the translation will be less laborious). For the Grecian is more according to my genius than the Latin poet. In the works of the two authors we may read their manners and natural inclinations, which are wholly different.

4. "*versus inopes rerum, nugaeque canorae*" (*Ars poetica*, l. 322).
5. Jeremy Collier, who in his *Short View of the Immorality and Profaneness of the English Stage* (1698) attacked many Restoration plays and dramatists, including Dryden.

Virgil was of a quiet, sedate temper: Homer was violent, impetuous, and full of fire. The chief talent of Virgil was propriety of thoughts, and ornament of words: Homer was rapid in his thoughts, and took all the liberties, both of numbers and of expressions, which his language, and the age in which he lived, allowed him: Homer's invention was more copious, Virgil's more confined: so that if Homer had not led the way, it was not in Virgil to have begun heroic poetry. For nothing can be more evident than that the Roman poem is but the second part of the *Ilias*, a continuation of the same story, and the persons already formed. The manners of Æneas are those of Hector, superadded to those which Homer gave him. The adventures of Ulysses in the *Odysseis* are imitated in the first six books of Virgil's *Æneis*; and though the accidents are not the same (which would have argued him of a servile copying, and total barrenness of invention), yet the seas were the same in which both the heroes wandered; and Dido cannot be denied to be the poetical daughter of Calypso. The six latter books of Virgil's poem are the four-and-twenty *Iliads* contracted: a quarrel occasioned by a lady, a single combat, battles fought, and a town besieged. I say not this in derogation to Virgil, neither do I contradict anything which I have formerly said in his just praise: for his episodes are almost wholly of his own invention, and the form which he has given to the telling makes the tale his own, even though the original story had been the same. But this proves, however, that Homer taught Virgil to design; and if invention be the first virtue of an epic poet, then the Latin poem can only be allowed the second place. Mr. Hobbes, in the preface to his own bald translation of the *Ilias* (studying poetry as he did mathematics, when it was too late), Mr. Hobbes, I say, begins the praise of Homer where he should have ended it. He tells us that the first beauty of an epic poem consists in diction, that is, in the choice of words, and harmony of numbers. Now, the words are the coloring of the work, which in the order of nature is last to be considered. The design, the disposition, the manners, and the thoughts, are all before it: where any of those are wanting or imperfect, so much wants or is imperfect in the imitation of human life, which is in the very definition of a poem. Words, indeed, like glaring colors, are the first beauties that arise and strike the sight; but if the draught be false or lame, the figures ill disposed, the manners obscure or inconsistent, or the thoughts unnatural, then the finest colors are but daubing, and the piece is a beautiful monster at the best. Neither Virgil nor Homer were deficient in any of the former beauties; but in this last, which is expression, the Roman poet is at least equal to the Grecian, as I have said elsewhere; supplying the poverty of his language by his musical ear and by his diligence.

But to return: our two great poets, being so different in their tempers, one choleric and sanguine, the other phlegmatic and melancholic; that which makes them excel in their several ways is that each of them has followed his own natural inclination, as well in forming the design as in the execution of it. The very heroes show their authors: Achilles is hot, impatient, revengeful,

> restless, irascible, unyielding, fierce, etc.,[6]

Æneas patient, considerate, careful of his people, and merciful to his enemies; ever submissive to the will of Heaven,

> let us follow wherever the fates may take us.[7]

I could please myself with enlarging on this subject, but am forced to defer it to a fitter time. From all I have said, I will only draw this inference, that the action of Homer being more full of vigor than that of Virgil, according to the temper of the writer, is of consequence more pleasing to the reader. One warms you by degrees; the other sets you on fire all at once, and never intermits his heat. 'Tis the same difference which Longinus makes betwixt the effects of eloquence in Demosthenes and Tully; one persuades, the other commands. You never cool while you read Homer, even not in the second book (a graceful flattery to his countrymen); but he hastens from the ships, and concludes not that book till he has made you an amends by the violent playing of a new machine. From thence he hurries on his action with variety of events, and ends it in less compass than two months. This vehemence of his, I confess, is more suitable to my temper; and, therefore, I have translated his

6. "*impiger, iracundus, inexorabilis, acer, etc.*" (Horace, *Ars poetica*, l. 121).
7. "*quo fata trahunt retrahuntque, sequamur*" (*Aeneid*, V. 709).

first book with greater pleasure than any part of Virgil. But it was not a pleasure without pains: the continual agitations of the spirits must needs be a weakening of any constitution, especially in age; and many pauses are required for refreshment betwixt the heats; the *Iliad* of itself being a third part longer than all Virgil's works together.

This is what I thought needful in this place to say of Homer. I proceed to Ovid and Chaucer, considering the former only in relation to the latter. With Ovid ended the golden age of the Roman tongue: from Chaucer the purity of the English tongue began. The manners of the poets were not unlike: both of them were well-bred, well-natured, amorous, and libertine, at least in their writings, it may be also in their lives. Their studies were the same, philosophy and philology. Both of them were knowing in astronomy, of which Ovid's books of the *Roman Feasts*, and Chaucer's *Treatise of the Astrolabe*, are sufficient witnesses. But Chaucer was likewise an astrologer, as were Virgil, Horace, Persius, and Manilius. Both writ with wonderful facility and clearness; neither were great inventors: for Ovid only copied the Grecian fables, and most of Chaucer's stories were taken from his Italian contemporaries, or their predecessors. Boccaccio his *Decameron* was first published, and from thence our Englishman has borrowed many of his *Canterbury Tales*: yet that of *Palamon and Arcite* was written in all probability by some Italian wit, in a former age, as I shall prove hereafter. The tale of Griselda was the invention of Petrarch; by him sent to Boccaccio, from whom it came to Chaucer. *Troilus and Cressida* was also written by a Lombard author, but much amplified by our English translator, as well as beautified;[8] the genius of our countrymen in general being rather to improve an invention than to invent themselves; as is evident not only in our poetry, but in many of our manufactures. I find I have anticipated already, and taken up from Boccaccio before I come to him: but there is so much less behind; and I am of the temper of most kings, who love to be in debt, are all for present money, no matter how they pay it afterwards. Besides, the nature of a preface is rambling, never wholly out of the way, nor in it.

8. Dryden was unaware that Boccaccio was Chaucer's source for both "The Knight's Tale" ("Palamon and Arcite") and *Troilus and Cressida*.

This I have learned from the practice of honest Montaigne, and return at my pleasure to Ovid and Chaucer, of whom I have little more to say.

Both of them built on the inventions of other men; yet since Chaucer had something of his own, as *The Wife of Bath's Tale*, *The Cock and the Fox*, which I have translated, and some others, I may justly give our countryman the precedence in that part; since I can remember nothing of Ovid which was wholly his. Both of them understood the manners: under which name I comprehend the passions and, in a larger sense, the descriptions of persons, and their very habits. For an example, I see Baucis and Philemon as perfectly before me, as if some ancient painter had drawn them; and all the Pilgrims in the *Canterbury Tales*, their humours, their features, and the very dress, as distinctly as if I had supped with them at the Tabard in Southwark. Yet even there, too, the figures of Chaucer are much more lively, and set in a better light; which though I have not time to prove, yet I appeal to the reader, and am sure he will clear me from partiality.

The thoughts and words remain to be considered, in the comparison of the two poets, and I have saved myself one half of that labor by owning that Ovid lived when the Roman tongue was in its meridian; Chaucer, in the dawning of our language: therefore that part of the comparison stands not on an equal foot, any more than the diction of Ennius and Ovid, or of Chaucer and our present English. The words are given up, as a post not to be defended in our poet, because he wanted the modern art of fortifying. The thoughts remain to be considered; and they are to be measured only by their propriety; that is, as they flow more or less naturally from the persons described, on such and such occasions. The vulgar judges, which are nine parts in ten of all nations, who call conceits and jingles wit, who see Ovid full of them, and Chaucer altogether without them, will think me little less than mad for preferring the Englishman to the Roman. Yet, with their leave, I must presume to say that the things they admire are only glittering trifles, and so far from being witty that in a serious poem they are nauseous, because they are unnatural. Would any man, who is ready to die for love, describe his passion like Narcissus? Would he think of "my wealth makes me poor,"[9] and a dozen more of such expressions, poured on the neck of one another, and signifying all the same thing? If this were wit, was this a time to be witty, when the poor wretch was in the agony of death? This is just John Littlewit, in *Bartholomew Fair*, who had a conceit (as he tells you) left him in his misery; a miserable conceit. On these occasions the poet should endeavor to raise pity: but instead of this, Ovid is tickling you to laugh. Virgil never made use of such machines when he was moving you to commiserate the death of Dido: he would not destroy what he was building. Chaucer makes Arcite violent in his love, and unjust in the pursuit of it; yet when he came to die, he made him think more reasonably: he repents not of his love, for that had altered his character; but acknowledges the injustice of his proceedings, and resigns Emilia to Palamon. What would Ovid have done on this occasion? He would certainly have made Arcite witty on his death-bed. He had complained he was farther off from possession, by being so near, and a thousand such boyisms, which Chaucer rejected as below the dignity of the subject. They who think otherwise would, by the same reason, prefer Lucan and Ovid to Homer and Virgil, and Martial to all four of them. As for the turn of words, in which Ovid particularly excels all poets, they are sometimes a fault, and sometimes a beauty, as they are used properly or improperly; but in strong passions always to be shunned, because passions are serious, and will admit no playing. The French have a high value for them; and I confess they are often what they call delicate, when they are introduced with judgment; but Chaucer writ with more simplicity, and followed nature more closely than to use them. I have thus far, to the best of my knowledge, been an upright judge betwixt the parties in competition, not meddling with the design nor the disposition of it; because the design was not their own; and in the disposing of it they were equal. It remains that I say somewhat of Chaucer in particular.

In the first place, as he is the father of English poetry, so I hold him in the same degree of veneration as the Grecians held Homer, or the Romans Virgil. He is a perpetual fountain of good sense; learned in all sciences; and therefore speaks properly on all subjects.

9. *"inopem me copia fecit"* (Ovid, *Metamorphoses*, III. 466).

As he knew what to say, so he knows also when to leave off; a continence which is practiced by few writers, and scarcely by any of the Ancients, excepting Virgil and Horace. One of our late great poets[10] is sunk in his reputation, because he could never forgive any conceit which came in his way; but swept like a dragnet, great and small. There was plenty enough, but the dishes were ill sorted; whole pyramids of sweetmeats for boys and women, but little of solid meat for men. All this proceeded not from any want of knowledge, but of judgment; neither did he want that in discerning the beauties and faults of other poets; but only indulged himself in the luxury of writing; and perhaps knew it was a fault, but hoped the reader would not find it. For this reason, though he must always be thought a great poet, he is no longer esteemed a good writer; and for ten impressions which his works have had in so many successive years, yet at present a hundred books are scarcely purchased once a twelve-month; for, as my last Lord Rochester said, though somewhat profanely, *Not being of God, he could not stand.*

Chaucer followed nature everywhere; but was never so bold to go beyond her; and there is a great difference of being "a poet" and "too much a poet," if we may believe Catullus,[11] as much as betwixt a modest behavior and affectation. The verse of Chaucer, I confess, is not harmonious to us; but 'tis like the eloquence of one whom Tacitus commends, it was "suited to the hearing of another age":[12] they who lived with him, and some time after him, thought it musical; and it continues so, even in our judgment, if compared with the numbers of Lydgate and Gower, his contemporaries: there is the rude sweetness of a Scotch tune in it, which is natural and pleasing, though not perfect. 'Tis true, I cannot go so far as he who published the last edition of him;[13] for he would make us believe the fault is in our ears, and that there were really ten syllables in a verse where we find but nine. But this opinion is not worth confuting;

10. Apparently Abraham Cowley, for whom Dryden himself had earlier had a high regard.

11. *"poeta . . . nimis poeta"* (Martial, III. 44. 4, not Catullus).

12. *"auribus istius temporis accommodata"* (*De oratoribus*, xxi).

13. Thomas Speght. Both Dryden and Speght were unaware of the stress upon final *e*'s in Middle English verse.

'tis so gross and obvious an error that common sense (which is a rule in everything but matters of faith and revelation) must convince the reader that equality of numbers in every verse which we call *heroic* was either not known, or not always practiced, in Chaucer's age. It were an easy matter to produce some thousands of his verses which are lame for want of half a foot, and sometimes a whole one, and which no pronunciation can make otherwise. We can only say that he lived in the infancy of our poetry, and that nothing is brought to perfection at the first. We must be children before we grow men. There was an Ennius, and in process of time a Lucilius, and a Lucretius, before Virgil and Horace; even after Chaucer there was a Spenser, a Harington, a Fairfax, before Waller and Denham were in being; and our numbers were in their nonage till these last appeared.

I need say little of his parentage, life and fortunes: they are to be found at large in all the editions of his works. He was employed abroad, and favored by Edward the Third, Richard the Second, and Henry the Fourth, and was poet, as I suppose, to all three of them. In Richard's time, I doubt, he was a little dipped in the rebellion of the Commons; and being brother-in-law to John of Gaunt, it was no wonder if he followed the fortunes of that family; and was well with Henry the Fourth when he had deposed his predecessor. Neither is it to be admired that Henry, who was a wise as well as a valiant prince, who claimed by succession, and was sensible that his title was not sound, but was rightfully in Mortimer, who had married the heir of York; it was not to be admired, I say, if that great politician should be pleased to have the greatest wit of those times in his interests, and to be the trumpet of his praises. Augustus had given him the example, by the advice of Maecenas, who recommended Virgil and Horace to him; whose praises helped to make him popular while he was alive, and after his death have made him precious to posterity.

As for the religion of our poet, he seems to have some little bias towards the opinions of Wycliffe, after John of Gaunt his patron; somewhat of which appears in the *Tale of Piers Plowman*.[14] Yet I

---

14. *Piers Plowman*, whose authorship is unknown, was regarded as Chaucer's in the seventeenth century. There is no evidence that Chaucer was a follower of Wycliffe or that he was related to John of Gaunt.

cannot blame him for inveighing so sharply against the vices of the clergy in his age: their pride, their ambition, their pomp, their avarice, their wordly interest, deserved the lashes which he gave them, both in that, and in most of his *Canterbury Tales*. Neither has his contemporary Boccaccio spared them. Yet both those poets lived in much esteem with good and holy men in orders; for the scandal which is given by particular priests reflects not on the sacred function. Chaucer's Monk, his Canon, and his Friar, took not from the character of his Good Parson. A satirical poet is the check of the laymen on bad priests. We are only to take care that we involve not the innocent with the guilty in the same condemnation. The good cannot be too much honored, nor the bad too coarsely used; for the corruption of the best becomes the worst. When a clergyman is whipped, his gown is first taken off, by which the dignity of his order is secured. If he be wrongfully accused, he has his action of slander; and 'tis at the poet's peril if he transgress the law. But they will tell us that all kind of satire, though never so well deserved by particular priests, yet brings the whole order into contempt. Is then the peerage of England anything dishonored when a peer suffers for his treason? If he be libeled, or any way defamed, he has his *scandalum magnatum* to punish the offender. They who use this kind of argument seem to be conscious to themselves of somewhat which has deserved the poet's lash, and are less concerned for their public capacity than for their private; at least there is pride at the bottom of their reasoning. If the faults of men in orders are only to be judged among themselves, they are all in some sort parties; for, since they say the honor of their order is concerned in every member of it, how can we be sure that they will be impartial judges? How far I may be allowed to speak my opinion in this case, I know not; but I am sure a dispute of this nature caused mischief in abundance betwixt a King of England and an Archbishop of Canterbury; one standing up for the laws of his land, and the other for the honor (as he called it) of God's Church; which ended in the murder of the prelate, and in the whipping of his Majesty from post to pillar for his penance. The learned and ingenious Dr. Drake[15] has saved me the labor of inquiring into the

15. James Drake, whose reply to Collier, *The Ancient and Modern Stages Surveyed* (1699), had recently been published.

esteem and reverence which the priests have had of old; and I would rather extend than dimish any part of it: yet I must needs say that when a priest provokes me without any occasion given him, I have no reason, unless it be the charity of a Christian, to forgive him: "self-defense"[16] is justification sufficient in the civil law. If I answer him in his language, self-defense, I am sure, must be allowed me; and if I carry it farther, even to a sharp recrimination, somewhat may be indulged to human frailty. Yet my resentment has not wrought so far, but that I have followed Chaucer in his character of a holy man, and have enlarged on that subject with some pleasure, reserving to myself the right, if I shall think fit hereafter, to describe another sort of priests, such as are more easily to be found than the Good Parson; such as have given the last blow to Christianity in this age, by a practice so contrary to their doctrine. But this will keep cold till another time.

In the meanwhile, I take up Chaucer where I left him. He must have been a man of a most wonderful comprehensive nature, because, as it has been truly observed of him, he has taken into the compass of his *Canterbury Tales* the various manners and humours (as we now call them) of the whole English nation in his age. Not a single character has escaped him. All his pilgrims are severally distinguished from each other; and not only in their inclinations, but in their very physiognomies and persons. Baptista Porta[17] could not have described their natures better than by the marks which the poet gives them. The matter and manner of their tales, and of their telling, are so suited to their different educations, humours, and callings, that each of them would be improper in any other mouth. Even the grave and serious characters are distinguished by their several sorts of gravity: their discourses are such as belong to their age, their calling, and their breeding; such as are becoming of them, and of them only. Some of his persons are vicious, and some virtuous; some are unlearned, or (as Chaucer calls them) *lewd*, and some are learned. Even the ribaldry of the low characters is different: the Reeve, the Miller, and the Cook, are several men, and distinguished from each other as much as the

16. "*prior laesit*" (Terence, *Eunuch*, prol. 6).
17. Giambattista della Porta, an Italian Renaissance physician and writer.

mincing Lady Prioress and the broad-speaking, gap-toothed Wife
of Bath. But enough of this: there is such a variety of game springing
up before me that I am distracted in my choice, and know not
which to follow. 'Tis sufficient to say, according to the proverb,
that here is God's plenty. We have our forefathers and great
grand-dames all before us, as they were in Chaucer's days: their
general characters are still remaining in mankind, and even in
England, though they are called by other names than those of
Monks, and Friars, and Canons, and Lady Abbesses, and Nuns;
for mankind is ever the same, and nothing lost out of nature, though
everything is altered. May I have leave to do myself the justice
(since my enemies will do me none, and are so far from granting
me to be a good poet that they will not allow me so much as to be
a Christian, or a moral man), may I have leave, I say, to inform my
reader that I have confined my choice to such tales of Chaucer as
savor nothing of immodesty. If I had desired more to please than
to instruct, the Reeve, the Miller, the Shipman, the Merchant,
the Summoner, and, above all, the Wife of Bath, in the Prologue
to her Tale, would have procured me as many friends and readers
as there are beaux and ladies of pleasure in the town. But I will no
more offend against good manners: I am sensible as I ought to be
of the scandal I have given by my loose writings; and make what
reparation I am able, by this public acknowledgment. If anything
of this nature, or of profaneness, be crept into these poems, I am so
far from defending it that I disown it. *Totum hoc indictum volo* [I wish
all such things had been unsaid]. Chaucer makes another manner of
apology for his broad speaking, and Boccaccio makes the like; but
I will follow neither of them. Our countryman, in the end of his
characters before the *Canterbury Tales*, thus excuses the ribaldry,
which is very gross in many of his novels:

> But first, I pray you, of your courtesy,
> That ye ne arrete it not my villany,
> Though that I plainly speak in this mattere,
> To tellen you her words, and eke her chere:
> Ne though I speak her words properly,
> For this ye knowen as well as I,
> Who shall tellen a tale after a man,

> He mote rehearse as nye as ever he can:
> Everich word of it ben in his charge,
> *All speke he, never so rudely, ne large:*
> Or else he mote tellen his tale untrue,
> Or feine things, or find words new:
> He may not spare, altho he were his brother,
> He mote as wel say o word as another.
> *Christ* spake himself full broad in holy writ,
> And well I wote no villany is it.
> Eke *Plato* saith, who so can him rede,
> The words mote been cousin to the dede.[18]

Yet if a man should have enquired of Boccaccio or of Chaucer what need they had of introducing such characters, where obscene words were proper in their mouths, but very undecent to be heard, I know not what answer they could have made: for that reason, such tales shall be left untold by me. You have here a specimen of Chaucer's language which is so obsolete that his sense is scarce to be understood; and you have likewise more than one example of his unequal numbers, which were mentioned before. Yet many of his verses consist of ten syllables, and the words not much behind our present English: as for example, these two lines in the description of the Carpenter's young wife:

> Wincing she was, as is a jolly colt,
> Long as a mast, and upright as a bolt.[19]

I have almost done with Chaucer, when I have answered some objections relating to my present work. I find some people are offended that I have turned these tales into modern English; because they think them unworthy of my pains, and look on Chaucer as a dry, old-fashioned wit, not worth receiving. I have often heard the late Earl of Leicester say that Mr. Cowley himself was of that opinion; who, having read him over at my Lord's request, declared he had no taste of him. I dare not advance my opinion against the judgment of so great an author: but I think it fair, however, to leave the decision to the public. Mr. Cowley was too modest to set up for a dictator; and being shocked perhaps with his old style, never

18. General Prologue, A. 725–742.
19. "The Miller's Tale," A. 3263–3264.

examined into the depth of his good sense. Chaucer, I confess, is a rough diamond, and must first be polished ere he shines. I deny not likewise that, living in our early days of poetry, he writes not always of a piece; but sometimes mingles trivial things with those of greater moment. Sometimes also, though not often, he runs riot, like Ovid, and knows not when he has said enough. But there are more great wits, beside Chaucer, whose fault is their excess of conceits, and those ill sorted. An author is not to write all he can, but only all he ought. Having observed this redundancy in Chaucer (as it is an easy matter for a man of ordinary parts to find a fault in one of greater) I have not tied myself to a literal translation; but have often omitted what I judged unnecessary, or not of dignity enough to appear in the company of better thoughts. I have presumed farther in some places, and added somewhat of my own where I thought my author was deficient, and had not given his thoughts their true luster, for want of words in the beginning of our language. And to this I was the more emboldened, because (if I may be permitted to say it of myself) I found I had a soul congenial to his, and that I had been conversant in the same studies. Another poet, in another age, may take the same liberty with my writings; if at least they live long enough to deserve correction. It was also necessary sometimes to restore the sense of Chaucer, which was lost or mangled in the errors of the press. Let this example suffice at present: in the story of Palamon and Arcite where the Temple of Diana is described, you find these verses in all the editions of our author:

> There saw I *Danè* turned unto a tree,
> I mean not the goddess *Diane*,
> But *Venus* daughter, which that hight *Danè*.[20]

Which, after a little consideration, I knew was to be reformed into this sense, that *Daphne*, the daughter of Peneus, was turned into a tree. I durst not make thus bold with Ovid, lest some future Milbourne[21] should arise, and say I varied from my author because I understood him not.

20. "The Knight's Tale," A. 2062–2064.
21. Luke Milbourne, who had attacked Dryden's translation of Virgil.

But there are other judges who think I ought not to have translated Chaucer into English, out of a quite contrary notion: they suppose there is a certain veneration due to his old language; and that it is little less than profanation and sacrilege to alter it. They are farther of opinion that somewhat of his good sense will suffer in this transfusion, and much of the beauty of his thoughts will infallibly be lost, which appear with more grace in their old habit. Of this opinion was that excellent person whom I mentioned, the late Earl of Leicester, who valued Chaucer as much as Mr. Cowley despised him. My Lord dissuaded me from this attempt (for I was thinking of it some years before his death), and his authority prevailed so far with me as to defer my undertaking while he lived, in deference to him. Yet my reason was not convinced with what he urged against it. If the first end of a writer be to be understood, then, as his language grows obsolete, his thoughts must grow obscure:

> many things that have decayed will come to life again, and words now honored will fall into disuse if usage wills it so, usage to which belong the standard and law and rule of all speech.[22]

When an ancient word, for its sound and significancy, deserves to be revived, I have that reasonable veneration for antiquity to restore it. All beyond this is superstition. Words are not like landmarks, so sacred as never to be removed: customs are changed, and even statutes are silently repealed, when the reason ceases for which they were enacted. As for the other part of the argument, that his thoughts will lose of their original beauty by the innovation of words: in the first place, not only their beauty, but their being is lost, where they are no longer understood, which is the present case. I grant that something must be lost in all transfusion, that is, in all translations; but the sense will remain, which would otherwise be lost, or at least be maimed, when it is scarce intelligible, and that but to a few. How few are there who can read Chaucer so as to

22. *multa renascentur, quae nunc cecidere; cadentque*
    *quae nunc sunt in honore vocabula, si volet usus,*
    *quem penes arbitrium est et jus et norma loquendi.*
            Horace, *Ars poetica*, ll. 70–72.

understand him perfectly? And if imperfectly, then with less profit, and no pleasure. 'Tis not for the use of some old Saxon friends that I have taken these pains with him: let them neglect my version, because they have no need of it. I made it for their sakes who understand sense and poetry as well as they, when that poetry and sense is put into words which they understand. I will go farther, and dare to add that what beauties I lose in some places, I give to others which had them not originally: but in this I may be partial to myself; let the reader judge, and I submit to his decision. Yet I think I have just occasion to complain of them, who because they understand Chaucer, would deprive the greater part of their countrymen of the same advantage, and hoard him up, as misers do their grandam gold,[23] only to look on it themselves, and hinder others from making use of it. In sum, I seriously protest that no man ever had, or can have, a greater veneration for Chaucer than myself. I have translated some part of his works only that I might perpetuate his memory, or at least refresh it, amongst my country-men. If I have altered him anywhere for the better, I must at the same time acknowledge that I could have done nothing without him: *facile est inventis addere* [it is easy to add to what has already been invented] is no great commendation; and I am not so vain to think I have deserved a greater. I will conclude what I have to say of him singly, with this one remark: a lady of my acquaintance, who keeps a kind of correspondence with some authors of the fair sex in France, has been informed by them that Mademoiselle de Scudéry, who is as old as Sibyl, and inspired like her by the same god of poetry, is at this time translating Chaucer into modern French. From which I gather that he has been formerly translated into the old Provençal (for how she should come to understand old English, I know not). But the matter of fact being true, it makes me think that there is something in it like fatality; that after certain periods of time the fame and memory of great wits should be re-newed, as Chaucer is both in France and England. If this be wholly chance, 'tis extraordinary; and I dare not call it more, for fear of being taxed with superstition.

23. Hoarded wealth.

Boccaccio comes last to be considered who, living in the same age with Chaucer, had the same genius, and followed the same studies. Both writ novels, and each of them cultivated his mother tongue. But the greatest resemblance of our two modern authors being in their familiar style, and pleasing way of relating comical adventures, I may pass it over, because I have translated nothing from Boccaccio of that nature. In the serious part of poetry, the advantage is wholly on Chaucer's side; for though the Englishman has borrowed many tales from the Italian, yet it appears that those of Boccaccio were not generally of his own making, but taken from authors of former ages, and by him only modeled; so that what there was of invention in either of them may be judged equal. But Chaucer has refined on Boccaccio and has mended the stories which he has borrowed in his way of telling; though prose allows more liberty of thought, and the expression is more easy when unconfined by numbers. Our countryman carries weight, and yet wins the race at disadvantage. I desire not the reader should take my word; and therefore I will set two of their discourses on the same subject in the same light, for every man to judge betwixt them. I translated Chaucer first, and amongst the rest pitched on *The Wife of Bath's Tale*; not daring, as I have said, to adventure on her Prologue, because 'tis too licentious. There Chaucer introduces an old woman of mean parentage, whom a youthful knight of noble blood was forced to marry, and consequently loathed her. The crone being in bed with him on the wedding-night, and finding his aversion, endeavors to win his affection by reason, and speaks a good word for herself (as who could blame her?), in hope to mollify the sullen bridegroom. She takes her topics from the benefits of poverty, the advantages of old age and ugliness, the vanity of youth, and the silly pride of ancestry and titles without inherent virtue, which is the true nobility. When I had closed Chaucer, I returned to Ovid and translated some more of his fables; and by this time had so far forgotten *The Wife of Bath's Tale* that when I took up Boccaccio, unawares I fell on the same argument of preferring virtue to nobility of blood and titles, in the story of Sigismonda; which I had certainly avoided, for the resemblance of the two discourses, if my memory had not failed me. Let the reader weigh them both; and if he thinks me partial to Chaucer, 'tis in him to right Boccaccio.

I prefer in our countryman, far above all his other stories, the noble poem of *Palamon and Arcite*, which is of the epic kind, and perhaps not much inferior to the *Ilias* or the *Æneis*: the story is more pleasing than either of them, the manners as perfect, the diction as poetical, the learning as deep and various, and the disposition full as artful: only it includes a greater length of time, as taking up seven years at least; but Aristotle has left undecided the duration of the action; which yet is easily reduced into the compass of a year, by a narration of what preceded the return of Palamon to Athens. I had thought for the honor of our nation, and more particularly for his, whose laurel, tho' unworthy, I have worn after him, that this story was of English growth, and Chaucer's own: but I was undeceived by Boccaccio; for, casually looking on the end of his seventh *Giornata*, I found Dioneo (under which name he shadows himself), and Fiametta (who represents his mistress, the natural daughter of Robert, King of Naples), of whom these words are spoken: "Dioneo and Fiametta told a long story of Arcita and Palemone";[24] by which it appears that this story was written before the time of Boccaccio; but the name of its author being wholly lost, Chaucer is now become an original; and I question not but the poem has received many beauties by passing through his noble hands. Besides this tale, there is another of his own invention, after the manner of the Provençals, called *The Flower and the Leaf*,[25] with which I was so particularly pleased, both for the invention and the moral, that I cannot hinder myself from recommending it to the reader.

As a corollary to this preface, in which I have done justice to others, I owe somewhat to myself: not that I think it worth my time to enter the lists with one M——, or one B——,[26] but barely to take notice that such men there are, who have written scurrilously

24. "*Dioneo e Fiametta gran pezza cantarono insieme d'Arcita, e di Palemone*" (*Decamerone*, VII. x, epilogue).

25. Uncertain authorship; in the seventeenth century the poem was attributed to Chaucer.

26. Luke Milbourne and Sir Richard Blackmore.

against me without any provocation. M——, who is in orders, pretends, amongst the rest, this quarrel to me, that I have fallen foul on priesthood. If I have, I am only to ask pardon of good priests, and am afraid his part of the reparation will come to little. Let him be satisfied that he shall not be able to force himself upon me for an adversary. I contemn him too much to enter into competition with him. His own translations of Virgil have answered his criticisms on mine. If (as they say he has declared in print) he prefers the version of Ogilby to mine, the world has made him the same compliment: for 'tis agreed on all hands that he writes even below Ogilby. That, you will say, is not easily to be done; but what cannot M—— bring about? I am satisfied, however, that, while he and I live together, I shall not be thought the worst poet of the age. It looks as if I had desired him underhand to write so ill against me; but upon my honest word I have not bribed him to do me this service, and am wholly guiltless of his pamphlet. 'Tis true I should be glad if I could persuade him to continue his good offices, and write such another critique on anything of mine; for I find by experience he has a great stroke with the reader, when he condemns any of my poems, to make the world have a better opinion of them. He has taken some pains with my poetry; but nobody will be persuaded to take the same with his. If I had taken to the Church (as he affirms, but which was never in my thoughts), I should have had more sense, if not more grace, than to have turned myself out of my benefice by writing libels on my parishioners. But his account of my manners and my principles are of a piece with his cavils and his poetry; and so I have done with him for ever.

As for the City Bard, or Knight Physician, I hear his quarrel to me is that I was the author of *Absalom and Achitophel*, which he thinks is a little hard on his fanatic patrons in London. But I will deal the more civilly with his two poems, because nothing ill is to be spoken of the dead: and therefore peace be to the Manes of his *Arthurs*.[27] I will only say that it was not for this noble Knight that I drew the plan of an epic poem on King Arthur in my preface to the translation of Juvenal. The Guardian Angels of kingdoms

---

27. Blackmore, a knight and Court Physician, was the author of two epics, *Prince Arthur* (1695) and *King Arthur* (1697).

were machines too ponderous for him to manage; and therefore he
rejected them, as Dares did the whirl-bats of Eryx when they were
thrown before him by Entellus. Yet from the preface he plainly
took his hint; for he began immediately upon the story, though he
had the baseness not to acknowledge his benefactor, but instead of
it to traduce me in a libel.

I shall say the less of Mr. Collier, because in many things he has
taxed me justly; and I have pleaded guilty to all thoughts and
expressions of mine which can be truly argued of obscenity, profaneness, or immorality, and retract them. If he be my enemy,
let him triumph; if he be my friend, as I have given him no personal
occasion to be otherwise, he will be glad of my repentance. It
becomes me not to draw my pen in the defense of a bad cause,
when I have so often drawn it for a good one. Yet it were not difficult
to prove that in many places he has perverted my meaning by his
glosses, and interpreted my words into blasphemy and bawdry,
of which they were not guilty. Besides that, he is too much given
to horseplay in his raillery, and comes to battle like a dictator from
the plough. I will not say, *The zeal of God's house has eaten him up*,[28]
but I am sure it has devoured some part of his good manners and
civility. It might also be doubted whether it were altogether zeal
which prompted him to this rough manner of proceeding; perhaps
it became not one of his function to rake into the rubbish of ancient
and modern plays; a divine might have employed his pains to
better purpose than in the nastiness of Plautus and Aristophanes,
whose examples, as they excuse not me, so it might be possibly
supposed that he read them not without some pleasure. They who
have written commentaries on those poets, or on Horace, Juvenal,
and Martial, have explained some vices, which without their
interpretation, had been unknown to modern times.

Neither has he judged impartially betwixt the former age and
us. There is more bawdry in one play of Fletcher's, called *The
Custom of the Country*, than in all ours together. Yet this has been
often acted on the stage in my remembrance. Are the times so
much more reformed now than they were five-and-twenty years ago?
If they are, I congratulate the amendment of our morals. But I

28. Psalms 69:9; John 2:17.

am not to prejudice the cause of my fellow-poets, though I abandon my own defense: they have some of them answered for themselves; and neither they nor I can think Mr. Collier so formidable an enemy that we should shun him. He has lost ground at the latter end of the day by pursuing his point too far, like the Prince of Condé at the battle of Senneph: from immoral plays to no plays, *ab abusu ad usum, non valet consequentia* [abuses do not have to lead to proper uses]. But, being a party, I am not to erect myself into a judge. As for the rest of those who have written against me, they are such scoundrels that they deserve not the least notice to be taken of them. B—— and M—— are only distinguished from the crowd by being remembered to their infamy:

> I order you, Demetrius and Tigellus, go and whine among your female students.[29]

"Preface," in *Fables Ancient and Modern; Translated into Verse, From Homer, Ovid, Boccace, & Chaucer: With Original Poems* (London: printed for Jacob Tonson, 1700), sigs. *A1–*D2v.

29.    *Demetri, teque, Tigelli,*
   *discipularum inter jubeo plorare cathedras.*
   Horace, *Satires*, I. x. 90–91.

# Selected Bibliography

CRANE, RONALD S. "English Neoclassical Criticism: An Outline Sketch." In *Critics and Criticism*, ed. Ronald S. Crane. Chicago: University of Chicago Press, 1952.

ELIOT, T. S. *John Dryden the Poet the Dramatist the Critic*. New York: Terence and Elsa Holliday, 1932.

FALLE, GEORGE G. "Dryden: Professional Man of Letters," *University of Toronto Quarterly*, XXVI (1957), 443–455.

JOHNSON, SAMUEL. "Life of Dryden." In *Lives of the English Poets*, ed. G. B. Hill. Oxford: Clarendon Press, 1905. Vol. I, pp. 331–481.

KER, W. P. Introduction to *Essays of John Dryden*. Oxford: Clarendon Press, 1900.

KIRSCH, ARTHUR C. *Dryden's Heroic Drama*. Princeton: Princeton University Press, 1965.

PRIOR, MOODY. "Poetic Drama: An Analysis and a Suggestion." In *English Institute Essays 1949*. New York: Columbia University Press, 1950. Pp. 3–32.

ROTHSTEIN, ERIC. "English Tragic Theory in the Late Seventeenth Century," *ELH*, XXIX (1962), 306–323.

SHERWOOD, JOHN C. "Dryden and the Rules: The Preface to the *Fables*," *Journal of English and Germanic Philology*, LII (1953), 13–26.

SMITH, R. JACK. "Shadwell's Impact upon John Dryden," *Review of English Studies*, XX (1944), 29–44.

TROWBRIDGE, HOYT. "The Place of Rules in Dryden's Criticism," *Modern Philology*, XLIV (1946), 84–96.

WARD, CHARLES E. *The Life of John Dryden*. Chapel Hill: University of North Carolina Press, 1961.

WATSON, GEORGE. "Introduction" to *John Dryden: Of Dramatic Poesy and Other Critical Essays*. London: J. M. Dent, 1962.

———. "Dryden's First Answer to Rymer," *Review of English Studies*, N.S. XIV (1963), 17–23.

WILLIAMSON, GEORGE. "The Occasion of *An Essay of Dramatic Poesy*," *Modern Philology*, XLIV (1946), 1–9.

# Index